Creating and Sustaining the Constructivist Classroom

Bruce A. Marlowe
Marilyn L. Page

CORWIN PRESS, INC.
A Sage Publications Company
Thousand Oaks, California

For information:

Corwin Press, Inc.
A Sage Publications Company
2455 Teller Road
Thousand Oaks, California 91320
E-mail: order@corwin.sagepub.com

SAGE Publications Ltd.
6 Bonhill Street
London EC2A 4PU
United Kingdom

SAGE Publications India Pvt. Ltd.
M-32 Market
Greater Kailash I
New Delhi 110 048 India

Printed in the United States of America

Library of Congress Cataloging-in-Publication Data

Marlowe, Bruce A.
    Creating and sustaining the constructivist classroom / by Bruce A.
Marlowe and Marilyn L. Page.
        p. cm.
    Includes bibliographical references and index.
    ISBN 0-8039-6587-7 (cloth: acid-free paper). — ISBN
0-8039-6588-5 (pbk.: acid-free paper)
    1. Constructivism (Education) 2. Active learning. 3. Teaching.
I. Page, Marilyn L. II. Title.
LB1590.3.M37 1997
370.15′2—dc21   97-33745

This book is printed on acid-free paper.

    00 01 02 03 10 9 8 7 6 5 4 3

Production Editor: Sherrise M. Purdum
Production Assistant: Denise Santoyo
Editorial Assistant: Kristen L. Gibson
Typesetter/Designer: Rebecca Evans
Indexer: Mary Mortensen
Cover Designer: Marcia M. Rosenburg
Print Buyer: Anna Chin

Contents

Preface

How We Got Here

Marilyn's Story

I started teaching secondary social studies in 1963, a time when schools were desperate for teachers and hired almost anyone, including me, who was breathing and had a bachelor's degree. I had no teacher training, had never had a course in education, and had never wanted to teach. I had to learn as I went along, and it was very slow learning. By 1984, I was preparing to leave teaching. I was bored, and the students were bored. Who cared about history anyway? Yes, students could memorize and recall historical information in my world history classes. They could discuss cause and effect; they could even draw conclusions, write decent essays, and participate in debates (all, of course, directed by me), but most of the students didn't really care about what they were doing.

Just before I was ready to resign, however, I read a newspaper article about students from another high school who were involved in a program called National History Day. It was the life and energy in the students' comments that caught my attention. I made a deal with myself, and probably with the devil, that I would teach for one more year and try having my students involved in this program. If I saw a difference, the deal went, I would give it one more year; if I saw no difference, I would leave teaching. Not that the next year was totally successful, but the differences in student attitude, engagement, understanding, accomplishment, application, and skill level were dramatic. As they say, the rest is history.

Unknowingly, what I had stumbled onto was an active learning program driven by constructivist propositions about learning. As I was to find out later in my research on the National History Day program, the folks involved in developing and running National History Day also were unaware of how their ideas on the teaching and learning of history connected to constructivist or any other education theory. In fact, none of the founders or directors of the program had ever taught at other than a college level.

One of the most important conclusions of the research was that learning that occurs when students own and are involved in inquiry, investigation, and discovery is different, more in-depth, more enduring, and much more powerful than what occurs in a traditional classroom. Translating this into learning experiences for teachers-in-training is a challenge. New and experienced teachers face an even greater challenge when they try to implement constructivist approaches in their classrooms, and that's how this book came to be.

I thought that the idea of an active learning experience as different from a directed lesson was something I stumbled upon myself until I recently realized that I had heard it all my life. My dad, a larger than life character, always supported any harebrained scheme my brothers, sister, and I concocted; he even encouraged us to create these ridiculous schemes. Whether a scheme worked or it didn't, it was always "quite a learning experience." Thanks, Dad.

Bruce's Story

Several years ago, I attended a workshop at which the keynote speaker, in an attempt to make a point about the rich connections between emotion and memory, asked members of the audience to recall, uncensored, the first thing that came to mind when they thought about 5th grade. Several workshop participants recounted embarrassing tales of spoiled lunches, or classmate teasing, or a variety of bathroom mishaps. There were other moments recalled as well, some joyous, others tragic, most merely the stuff of preadolescent melodrama. Although the emotional content of these memories was often highly charged, what was more fascinating to me about this exercise was the complete lack of responses related to what most of us in education like to believe school is about, despite the speaker's request for us to remember a specific grade- (not age-) related experience. No one said, "I remember learning about prepositions" or "I remember learning about Magellan's voyages" or "I remember learning how to add and subtract fractions." I have since repeated this exercise (using every grade level K-12) at other workshops, in my classes with undergraduate and graduate students, and when talking to groups of inservice teachers; virtually every response I have ever received follows the same pattern. In the 7 years that I have asked this question, only four individuals have ever recalled an experience related to school learning.

What came to my mind first at that initial workshop was sitting in Mrs. Butler's 5th grade classroom watching the clock and waiting. And watching others watching the clock and waiting. Waiting, staring, hoping for what seemed like an eternity for the bell to ring at the end of the day, between periods, before recess. In the 10th grade, but not before then, things changed dramatically. I entered a democratic public school program called School-Within-A-School (SWS) that treated students (100 of them between 10th and 12th grade) and teachers (3, plus a guidance counselor) as community members with equal rights and responsibilities. Students governed the program, established curriculum guidelines, determined which courses should be required and which could be taken only after the completion of prerequisites, settled disputes through a student court, gave grades, and taught courses. Suddenly school was exciting. I began to enjoy reading and writing and debating and thinking.

Ironically, when I first started teaching English in a high school for students with learning disabilities I forgot all of this. I was asked to teach from a text handed to me on my first day, and I did. I was asked to ensure that students were assigned 30 minutes of homework each night, and I did. I was asked to test students at the end of each week, and I did. As I watched my students watch the clock, I began to remember my own school experiences, and I realized that nothing I was being asked to do—nothing that my students or I were doing—had anything to do with learning English. I quickly switched gears.

For an extended investigation of propaganda, my students prepared questions—and rebuttals to predicted responses—for a variety of demonstrators who we would later visit in their semipermanent encampments on the Mall in Washington, D.C. Students interviewed aspiring politicians, militant animal rights activists, Vietnam veterans, individuals protesting U.S. foreign policy in El Salvador, and a host of others with strong views and sharp rhetoric. My students came alive in ways I was told students with learning disabilities could not. They debated with demonstrators, worked together to make videotape productions, recorded and analyzed the language and logic of the people they interviewed, and presented their findings to others in their class.

Where Are We Now?

During the last decade of working with student teachers and in-service teachers in a variety of K-12 settings, we have seen the same two problems connected to attempts to engage students actively in their own learning. These problems involve confusion over constructivist, active learning propositions and frustration with, and lack of support for, trying to create constructivist classrooms. We have written this practical guide to constructivism to help pre-service and in-service teachers understand the tenets of constructivism more clearly and to implement, more easily and effectively, constructivist approaches in the classroom. Mounting research, our own experiences as educators, and reports from pre-service and in-service teachers support our belief that constructivist, active learning programs not only are more engaging but also promote elaborate knowledge construction; encourage empowered, informed, and independent thinking and doing; foster deeper understanding of concepts; nourish more enduring learning; and lead to greater command and ownership of content.

Even when teachers recognize the value of and want to and try to use constructivist approaches in their classrooms, their efforts often produce less than what they expect. The first problem is that, although constructivist propositions can seem fairly simple, hundreds of observations of, and questions from, pre-service and in-service teachers over the past 10 years show that they are not. For example many teachers ask questions such as: What does it mean to have students construct their own knowledge? How is understanding different from recalling? What does it mean to have students demonstrate their understanding? What does past experience have to do with learning? Does constructivism mean students do what they want? If students are sitting in a circle, does that mean learning is constructivist?

The second problem is figuring out how to begin. Teachers ask: How can I change my classroom when the rest of the school stays the same? What if the students think it means they can do what they want? What can I do if the principal and other teachers don't even understand what constructivism means? How can I sustain a vision if the school board and community do not understand it?

How This Book Is Different From Others

There already is much written about theories of constructivism and the connection to superior learning results; however, there is no *consolidated* discussion of the foundations, results, and practical issues of constructivism. Additionally, there are few guidelines to help new or experienced teachers create and sustain a constructivist classroom. Our book does both. Our first purpose in writing this book is to bring together and clarify for educators the theoretical foundations and key issues pre-service and in-service teachers raise about creating and sustaining constructivist classrooms. The second purpose is to give educators the tools to make a mental and practical shift from a traditional to a constructivist format. We provide guidelines, practical tips, and models that will help teachers to implement related changes at any grade level. Checklists will help teachers determine where they are now, where they are going, and how they are doing along the way. Additionally, we include reports on attempts, successes, and problems from teachers at different grade levels, and from one special new teacher, Susan Jackson.

Why Now?

There are three reasons why this book is so necessary now. First, since the early 1980s, there has been an avalanche of literature supporting the need for the kind of active learning experiences described, advocated, and supported by constructivism. We know that a traditional educational system focusing mainly on a teacher or another student dispensing information is inadequate and inappropriate for the present and future needs of students. We also know that the issue is not as simple as jumping from one set of assumptions about teaching and learning to another, and we know that content is a crucial issue. In this book, we not only clarify the importance of content and standards as a key element in a constructivist class/program but also demonstrate how, when fully understood and implemented, constructivist approaches lead to greater command of content and a higher level of performance than does a traditional program.

Second, teachers and administrators already working with constructivist reform initiatives are feeling overwhelmed and need guidelines to help with implementation. These initiatives include new state documents on common cores of learning for grades K-12 and/or related curriculum framework guidelines such as are being or have been developed in Vermont, California, Massachusetts, Oregon, Pennsylvania, and Kentucky. Another set of initiatives comes from major research reports such as the Carnegie reports on middle and secondary education and from reform efforts of large national educational organizations such as the National Middle School Association and the national teacher organizations for math, science, English, and social studies. Teachers are struggling to assimilate all this new information and to put it into practice, more often than not with little or no training either in the necessary philosophical and theoretical foundations or in the practical how-to. Educators are scrambling to figure out what these recommendations mean and how to implement them. Their reactions are a frantic "Why? How? When? . . . HELP!"

The third reason people need help at this time is that no reforms will last or be effective if educators can't/don't make the necessary philosophical mind shift. Educators can make Band-Aid® changes; that is, they can move to block scheduling, they can let students choose a topic, they can use different seating arrangements, and they can try new instructional approaches. If, however, change is to be meaningful and more than superficial, they need also to change their set of assumptions about how people learn and what constitutes learning. They need, in fact, to redirect their focus from the concepts of teaching to the concepts of learning; this is not easy. Our book will help teachers to move step by step from their traditional worldview to a constructivist one. Always, it is grounded in the theoretical and research base of constructivism and the tenet "You can *teach* students anything, but it doesn't mean they have *learned* a thing."

The Book's Structure

We have, from the beginning, conceived of *Creating and Sustaining the Constructivist Classroom* as a working book; it is designed to be useful, and we expect and hope that your copy will be written in and dog-eared. Several of the chapters contain checklists and exercises, and almost all the chapters contain a section we call "Tough Questions." These questions are designed to provoke discussion and debate about the challenges and dilemmas active learning environments pose for pre- and in-service teachers and education professors.

We start the book with a cautionary tale about the dangers of trying to do too much too soon. In Chapter 1, "Armed and Dangerous," readers will meet Susan Jackson, a beginning teacher with big ideas. Chapter 2, "Back to the Future," reviews the historical roots of contemporary constructivism, provides a definition of constructivism, and describes the research-based rationale for creating the constructivist classroom. In "Coming of Age: The Active Learning Movement," our third chapter, we provide an overview of current educational reform efforts related to constructivism by grade levels; this includes clarification of the recommendations of professional organizations such as the NCTM, NSTA, NCTE, NCSS, and other organizations that develop national standards in the disciplines. In the fourth chapter, "Look Before You Leap," we begin with self-assessment checklists and then lay the groundwork for helping you create a constructivist classroom by asking you to reflect on your current practice with respect to student and teacher roles, classroom management issues, the communication system of your classroom, and the ways in which you assess student learning. "Back to the *Real Basics*", Chapter 5, begins with a look at the ways content learning is handled in constructivist as opposed to traditional classroom settings and then offers step-by-step suggestions for helping you to make changes in your classroom, communicate these changes to students and parents, and enlist the support of your principal and community. In Chapter 6, "Getting Your Feet Wet," we introduce three specific active learning models and practical steps you can implement right away to change your classroom to an active learning environment. In Chapter 7, "Diving In," teachers and students in different academic levels tell their stories.

The next two chapters address special issues related to the constructivist classroom. In Chapter 8, "Untangling the Web," we explore the potential of the use of technology and provide a framework for integrating current and future technologies in constructivist classrooms. "Making the Most of the Classroom Mosaic," Chapter 9, addresses the difficult issues connected to working in classrooms that include special education students, students from new immigrant and refugee groups, and the increasing number of students who live in poverty. Here you will find practical guidelines and tips for understanding and addressing these issues. We return in Chapter 10, "Redemption and Bon Voyage," to the beginning—for an update on Susan—and to the future as you begin or continue your own journey.

There are two issues in particular (in connection with creating a constructivist classroom) that need further examination, development, analysis, and clarification. These are the issues of whole system change and assessment goals and procedures. Although we recognize the importance of systemic change, we also know how effective one teacher can be, not only in helping students to learn in a different and more substantial way but also in generating colleague and school interest in the larger change process.

Although our book does not contain a specific section on the issue of system change, it does provide support and examples for teachers who want to make changes but, by necessity, have to make changes on their own and often in a less than accommodating environment. It helps teachers to identify, eliminate, work with, and avoid system barriers. It discusses other teachers' experiences, successes, questions, and problems, and it provides a way for teachers to stay focused and to move forward.

As for the issue of assessment, we (with the help of the teacher-contributors) address and frame various components and concerns in several chapters—particularly in Chapters 4, 6, 7, 8, and 9—and provide an assessment checklist in Chapter 4. To continue work on framing and clarifying both issues—system change and assessment—as well as other concerns related to developing constructivist classrooms, we invite you, the readers, to join us at our interactive web site, The International Center for Constructivist Classroom Teachers. Look at and join in conversations; submit plans, ideas, and problems; ask and respond to questions. This is our way of providing a network of support and exchange for teachers who are now involved or want to get involved in the kind of change we describe and advocate in our book. Through this communication, perhaps together we will all write a sequel to *Creating and Sustaining the Constructivist Classroom*.

Acknowledgments

When we first began writing this book, Peter Spitzform, reference librarian at Johnson State College, volunteered his assistance. He couldn't have imagined how much we would be asking him to do. He was there for us not only in locating and retrieving sources of all kinds in the midst of our writing but also, when we were both out of the state and needed much help in checking reference citations, he devoted complete days and weeks to helping us. We could not have met editing deadlines without him. A simple thank you seems totally inadequate.

Even before we began writing, Jon Margerum-Leys and Peter Weinstein, contributors to Chapter 8, asked us extremely challenging questions about where we were headed. Several scholars and educators read early versions of the manuscript. We want to give special thanks to Grace Brown, Robert Ferrell, Pam Galvani, Robert Mackin, Robert McCarthy, Robert Smith, and Patrick Sullivan. Their questions and ideas were extremely valuable and helped to shape this book.

Three reviewers—Alfie Kohn, James Beane, and Don Christensen—deserve special mention; each provided detailed critiques, useful suggestions, and considerable encouragement. In addition, Don Christensen persuaded us to end each chapter with "tough questions" that would give readers the opportunity to analyze and pursue their own issues.

It was our good fortune that several highly skilled teachers helped in the preparation of this book. You will hear from Katy Smith, "Susan Jackson," "Jan Carpenter," Ann Lipsitt, and Janette Roberts in the body of the book. Along with Dianne Quinn and Kim Hauge, these teachers not only demonstrated the power of constructivist teaching but also offered much useful feedback while the manuscript was in progress. We also want to thank all the teachers and student teachers with whom we have worked and spoken. They have always been our inspirations. Here in the Department of Education at Johnson State College, where we prepared most of the book, we work with an outstanding group of educators who deserve individual mention: Annamary Anderson, Ken Brighton, Robert DiGiulio, Carol Story, Herb Tilley, Alice Whiting, and Darlene Witte. These colleagues, each of whom is committed to excellence in teacher education, continually and willingly gave their time to review the manuscript and provided us with the ideal forum for "fleshing out" many of our ideas. We cannot thank them enough for their expertise, advice, questions, support, and good humor.

Additionally, we want to recognize John Towne, our resident computer expert, who saved us from ourselves, and Vincent Crockenberg, our Academic Dean, who provided continuous encouragement and support. For understanding what we wanted to do and for supporting us from the beginning, we give immeasurable thanks to our family members—Pam Rush, Rachel Rush-Marlowe, Dave Page, Phil Page, and Jeannie Page. A special thanks goes to Fran Parsons, who has always been there. We thank all our friends for bearing with us and helping us in many different ways. Thanks also to colleagues not mentioned above, especially to Dave Hutchinson, who asked us if we were still speaking to each other after writing a book together. The answer is a resounding "yes." Dave helped us clarify what an amazing, collaborative journey this has been.

Finally, we owe a special thanks to Alice Foster, our editor at Corwin Press, who guided us through the publishing process from the very beginning. Although any faults contained in this book are ours alone, it was Alice's tough questions, her clear and compelling feedback, and her ability to keep our thinking focused that ultimately allowed our ideas to become a book. Thanks also to Sherrise Purdum, our production editor, who kept us on track and on time, yet was flexible when we needed some leeway. A. J. Sobczak, our copy editor, was simply outstanding. His attention to detail and his ability to deal with us, our reference librarian Peter Spitzform, and a multitude of simultaneous e-mail messages was nothing short of remarkable.

About the Authors

Bruce A. Marlowe earned his PhD in educational psychology from The Catholic University of America in Washington, D.C., and completed 2 years of postdoctoral training in neuropsychology with Dr. William Stixrud. Currently, he is Associate Professor of Education at Johnson State College in Vermont and co-director of The Learning Co-op, which provides diagnostic testing and educational consulting services to children and their families. He began his 15-year career in education at the Center for Unique Learners in Rockville, Maryland, where he served as a teacher and a school consultant. He has taught at the elementary, secondary, and college levels, and he is a frequent presenter at teacher training workshops and academic conferences. He lives in north-central Vermont with his wife and daughter.

Marilyn L. Page is Associate Professor of Education at Johnson State College in Johnson, Vermont. She began her career in education in 1963 as a high school social studies teacher and has taught in every grade from 7th to 12th, at every academic level, in rural, suburban, and urban school systems. She received her EdD from the University of Massachusetts in Amherst in Instructional Leadership: Secondary Teacher Education and in Educational Media and Instructional Technology. At Johnson State College, she has developed the Middle School Teacher Education Program and is currently serving as technology coordinator for teacher education programs. She consults on reform issues, social studies education, and technology in education. She lives in Johnson, Vermont, and in Wrentham, Massachusetts.

To reach Marilyn Page or Bruce Marlowe by mail, contact Johnson State College, Johnson, VT 05656.

Telephone: Bruce Marlowe, (802) 635-1472
            Marilyn Page, (802) 635-1408

E-mail: Marloweb@badger.jsc.vsc.edu
            Pagem@badger.jsc.vsc.edu

Internet: International Center for Constructivist Classroom
            Teachers—under construction as a link to Johnson
            State College

To the memory of Avish and Nancy Dworkin, who inspired great teaching, and to Gene Chiaverini and Bonnie McClellan, who showed me how to make it happen.

—B. M.

To the memory of my father, Norman Monks, who through example and words always encouraged me to think wildly, and to my mother, Mabel Monks, who always asked (and in doing so taught me about) critical questions. To Dave, Phil, and Jeannie for being who they are.

—M. P.

One

Armed and Dangerous

A Cautionary Tale

As professors whose primary experience at the college level has been in teacher education programs, we have had the opportunity to teach and learn with hundreds of prospective teachers. Many leave their training with an almost palpable zeal for change. Unfortunately, enthusiasm, strong teaching skills, and even a love for students and learning are not enough. Making change, any change, is slow, sometimes painful, and exponentially more difficult as the number of people one wants to include in the change process increases . . . which is why we begin this book with a cautionary tale about the peril of banking on achieving too much too soon.

Susan Jackson

One of our best students, a young woman named "Susan Jackson" (a pseudonym), was as excited about teaching as anyone either of us can remember. Susan was a crackerjack student. She was dynamic, engaging, and highly inquisitive. She was interested not only in how things worked in educational settings but also in *why* the pieces fit together the way they did. Her curiosity was contagious. In fact, of all the students we have known, Susan stood out in terms of both her intellectual curiosity and her enthusiasm—enviable traits for a teacher charged with actively engaging students in learning. Susan also was among the very strongest students we had in terms of her ability to grasp theoretical issues, articulate her arguments, and integrate theory with practice. Finally, she had excellent writing and verbal

1

communication skills, and by the time she graduated, Susan had ac-
cumulated a solid repertoire of very creative ideas about how to help
students develop these important skills. In short, Susan represented
the best our system has to offer, and in many ways she seemed like
a perfect candidate for becoming a strong change agent as well.

Susan's story is a common one. Armed, ready, and excited for constructivist teaching, she found herself surrounded by teachers who
simply did not see things her way and students unprepared to play
along . . . but we're getting ahead of ourselves. Let's start at the beginning with Susan's culminating college experience of working in a
9th grade English classroom. Here is what Susan had to say about
what her "dream school" would look like shortly before her culminating project began.

Susan's Ideal World

*In my ideal world, I will graduate and get a well-paying teaching job at a prog-
ressive school where the students and teachers are self-motivated—where
teachers, administrators, and students work together to create exciting, fascinating, fun learning experiences. The best part of working in my dream school
though, is that it is filled with problem solving yes-sayers rather than griping
nay-sayers. When an exciting or unusual opportunity for learning presents itself, the members of my school community will get together and say, "We really
must find a way to make this happen," rather than, "Oh we couldn't possibly
do that because. . . ." In addition, I want to be in a school just to be in a school.
I want to sit at a lunch table with good teachers who care about their students
and just listen to what they have to say. I want to be in a place where I can ask
more than one teacher, "This is what happened to me today. What would you
do in this situation?" I want to see for myself what it is like to have 5 special
needs students in a class of 20. I want to hear the kinds of things that teachers
gripe about in low voices during free periods in the day.*

Susan's Experience at the High School

As Susan would later discover, high school freshmen, classrooms,
and schools are often significantly shy of her dream. Nevertheless,
Susan had the good fortune of working with a teacher who was open
to new ideas, ready for some experimentation, and willing to follow

Susan's lead for at least one major project. The excerpt below comes from Susan's self-evaluation of her culminating experience.

One of the first questions I asked Marcia (the cooperating teacher) was, "How much freedom do we have in terms of what the students can explore, how they go about doing it, and how they show us what they have learned?" She explained that the school had already decided that all 9th grade students would do a unit on Greek mythology. She said that this had been the case for several years. She explained the ways in which she had taught the topic in the past but said that she was willing to try a new approach. From what I gathered, her approach in the past was fairly "traditional." As I understood it, she had the class begin with the Greek story of the creation of the earth, which the whole class read and discussed together. She then had them move into the "hero" stories and then moved on to several of the other well-known myths. She said that in the past she gave weekly quizzes on vocabulary and content, and ended the unit with a comprehensive exam. In other words, Marcia's approach in the past had been to try to expose each student to several (and all the same) of the Greek myths, and to discuss some of the broad themes like the "role of the hero in Greek mythology."

The approach I advocated was a bit different. The model I used was basically the model used in many of my college classes. I suggested that each student, either alone or with a partner, pick a myth, a mythological character, or some other aspect of Greek culture and create an original exhibition to present to the class. Using this approach, each student would have the opportunity to become an "expert" on some aspect of Greek culture or mythology and, because they had to present to the entire class, all of the students would be exposed to every topic. Marcia said that she liked the idea of projects, although she also said that she had never given the students total freedom in choosing their topics, and she was interested to see how well they would handle it.

For my first lesson, I introduced myself, told them a bit about my philosophy of learning, and explained to the class that I needed their help. I needed to know what they thought were the qualities of a good teacher. We spent the rest of the period generating this list. For their homework assignment, Marcia asked the students to pick the two or three qualities they thought were most important and to explain why these qualities were at the top of their personal lists. In addition, I asked the students to write me a short letter that began, "Dear Miss Jackson, one thing I liked about today's class was that . . . and one thing I did not like or did not understand about today's class was that . . ." The letters were a wonderful way to begin to get to know the students. I could also begin to identify which students were willing to take some time to think about the question and which students just wrote something down to get it over with.

The next step in this process was to try to determine what the students already knew about the Greeks and Greek mythology. In addition, I wanted the students to begin thinking about ways they could demonstrate their understanding of a topic other than by taking a test or writing an essay. We spent the last half of the class talking about what authentic assessment means. We generated another list, similar to the good teacher list, and I gave each student a copy. Following these discussions I struggled with the following questions:

How do I get them to understand what a great project looks like?

What would be a good way to have students tell me what they are thinking of exploring for their exhibitions?

How will I know if my expectations are clear?

How can I make sure that the students are actually doing something productive and moving forward, and not just goofing off in the library?

I came up with the idea of an update sheet. I asked the students to fill out an update sheet during the last few minutes of each class period. I intended to look over the sheets at the end of each day to try to assess where each student was in the process and to help me pinpoint students who might need my help finding resources. Approximately 2 weeks into the project, I asked the students to fill out a final contract telling me exactly what they had planned to do for their exhibitions. I also gave the students a document that explained the criteria (which they helped develop) on which they would be evaluated. Attached to the evaluation sheet was a calendar which showed the students which days they were scheduled to present.

Overall, the presentations went well. Many of the students' exhibitions were exceptional. Some of the students made video- and audiotapes. Others wrote and performed original monologues in costume. One student made an incredibly lifelike clay sculpture of Hercules slaying the Hydra. After the student's presentation, the principal asked if he could display the statue in the center of the front hall. Two students even researched the eating habits of the ancient Greeks and cooked an ancient Greek feast for the entire class. While we ate, our chefs used a map they had created to explain the ancient Greeks' trade routes and the origins of the products they bartered.

Preparing for the Real World

Susan's experience was, in many ways, both transformative and validating. She had learned about constructivist approaches in her college classes and had a positive and successful experience trying them out. As she prepared for her first full-time teaching job in the Northwest, where she was hired as a member of a middle school team specifically to nudge some of the older teachers toward more progressive practice, the following questions, which she created as part of her culminating college experience, guided her:

> *How can I facilitate students' learning in such a way that I provide opportunities for them to discover, create, and apply knowledge for themselves while working within a public school setting?*
>
> *How can I get students to push themselves beyond what they dreamed they were capable of?*
>
> *How can I get them to want to truly understand what they learn and to demonstrate that understanding in a meaningful and creative way, rather than just memorizing information and spitting it back out on a test?*
>
> *How do I get students to understand that learning for learning's sake is cool, and fun, and hard, and much more worthwhile than memorizing information for a grade and then forgetting it?*

The Reality

These are tough questions, but Susan, buoyed by her successful culminating experience, a long summer break, and the confidence of a much more experienced teacher, felt ready to tackle them head-on. What she found when she arrived was anything but what she expected. By October of her first year of teaching, six short weeks into the semester, Susan sent us the following poem.

The Poem

I Hate—A Poem by a First-Year Teacher

I hate preparing lessons.
I hate that feeling of panic of "what am I going to do tomorrow?"
I hate vomiting in the morning.
I hate kids who try to slime out of doing things like Steve and Billy do.
I hate getting up at five o'clock (or four-forty-five, or four-thirty).

I hate it when Pamela reminds me of Stacy Jefferson, the girl who made my life hell in 7th grade.

I hate it when Elizabeth Milios yells at a kid who is crying because he is having problems with his ex-girlfriend.

I hate it when Cindy Tuppan looks at me with that bitchy smirk and I know she would secretly love to see me fail.

I hate territorial teachers.

I hate feeling incompetent.

I hate crying when I feel like this.

I hate not having any friends here.

I hate feeling lost.

I hate it when a fourteen-year-old can make me feel exactly the way I felt when I was fourteen years old.

I hate it when kids talk when I am trying to tell them something.

I hate it more when kids who were talking ask me, "Now what are we supposed to do?"

I hate Fridays because that means Monday is only three days away.

I hate Sundays because that means Monday is tomorrow.

What happened? Could this be the same Susan Jackson who left our program so confident, determined, and excited about teaching? By November, things had not improved. Another letter, this one more urgent, followed.

The Letter

Last Monday was definitely the lowest point in my life. We had a great in-service. We had to sit at tables with our "teammates" and he told us all about the kinds of things that he has done with interdisciplinary units, and he showed us how to start with a topic that middle school kids are interested in and then make a web of related topics, etc. Things were going well, overall. After lunch, we met with him as grade level teachers for about an hour, and he asked us to voice concerns that we had with our particular students. It was then that I realized how little faith the teachers at this school have in the students at our school. They truly don't believe that the kids have any desire to learn. They really believe that the kids have to be bribed to do anything.

So after we met with him, we were supposed to go upstairs as a team and brainstorm ideas about ways we might be able to do an interdisciplinary unit ourselves. So . . . I got upstairs and John (the social studies teacher who only lectures and teaches straight out of the social studies textbook) was sitting at his desk, and I said, "So do you want to meet in here?" At the same moment, Cindy Tuppan (a science teacher) walked in and John said, "Yeah—whatever. Do we even need to meet? What's the point? I'll tell you what we could do. We could just sit here and pretend to be meeting in case Mr. Schwartz (the principal) walks by—or we could just leave." I had no idea what to say.

Then Cindy said, "Well, I can't do this. I can't teach like this. I'm a science teacher. I can't teach a unit on freedom" (the topic we had been webbing in the in-service as an example). "There is absolutely no place for science in anything we were talking about down there. I can't teach like that."

And I lost it.

I felt all the frustration come up from the pit of my stomach, and I said something like, "Well Cindy I know how you feel . . ." (and the tears started flowing). "I feel so frustrated every day because that was the way I learned to teach. I wasn't trained to teach from a textbook. Every day I feel so %@#* frustrated . . ." (I'm not sure if that was where I said %@#*, but I said it) "because I feel like I was hired to teach here because I do know how to teach like that, but nobody else in this place, or at least on this team, teaches like that or even wants to teach like that and I hate it!"

At some point during this outburst, Elizabeth Milios walked in and said, "Well, then maybe you're in the wrong place! But don't you start blaming the team. It is not the team's fault. There are plenty of people in this school who would love to be on this team!"

Then Cindy pipes in with this: "Your insecurities and your inabilities are not my problem. You are not my problem. I don't care about your problems. I don't care about you."

Ahh, yes, teaming at its finest. At some point I told Elizabeth not to yell at me like I was one of her students. I did stop crying, but I literally felt like someone had dropped a barbell on my stomach. The rest of the day is a fog. We had to go down to the library to wrap things up. Everything in my whole being wanted to run away from that place. At the end of the in-service, one of the other new teachers, Reggie, looked at me and said, "Are you all right?" I looked at him and shook my head no, but I couldn't speak.

He said, "Come to my room." I followed him out of the library and the tears just started pouring out of my eyes.

We got to his room and I started sobbing and I kept saying, "I can't do this. I can't do this. I thought I could but I can't. I have to resign. This is killing me. I can't do this."

Reggie just sat there on his knees and listened to me and he kept saying, "Don't quit. Don't quit. I'll help you. We'll do it together, whatever it takes. I swear I'll help you. You are meant to be a teacher."

What Will Happen? What Did Happen?

Three months after beginning what promised to be a stellar teaching career, Susan Jackson found herself, crying on the floor of an 8th grade public classroom, at a crossroads. Should she forge ahead or quit? Was the enthusiasm and energy, her love for teaching, knocked out of her so early in the game? What went wrong?

We share this story not to discourage current or future teachers but to generate thinking and to raise questions by all involved in the teaching profession. Was Susan's teacher preparation program inadequate? Were her goals too lofty? Were the teachers in Susan's school woefully uninformed or inflexible? Was Susan expecting too much? How typical is Susan's experience?

We will return to Susan's story later, but before we do, we need to examine the foundation upon which Susan's teaching was built. Where did she get all those crazy ideas about interdisciplinary thematic units and active student involvement, about inquiry-based learning and problem solving, about student-designed curriculum and student-driven assessment? Where did these ideas come from? Are they new? Progressive? Or are these ideas old, maybe even very old?

Read on . . .

Two

Back to the Future

This chapter looks at the origins of, and support for, Susan's ideas. We define constructivism, review the historical grounding and research that support constructivism, and look at the myths that surround constructivist classrooms. One purpose of this chapter is to demonstrate that Susan had centuries of philosophical, theoretical, and practical backing for what she considered the *real basics*. (We will discuss other issues relating to Susan's experience throughout the book.) Another purpose is to provide the rationale for you to create a successful constructivist classroom and to encourage you to generate the powerful and critical questions that will lead you to positive, productive, and practical action.

What Exactly Is Constructivism?

It's About Constructing Knowledge, Not Receiving It

Constructivism is a theory about how we learn. If you were to write a definition or theory of learning, what would that be? What would be the core concepts? Would your definition be related to evaluation of a student's work? Would you describe learning in relation to a student's behavior or recitation? Would you relate it to your teaching? How would you—how do you—know when your students have learned? Would someone observing your classes be able to recognize learning as it occurred? Here is Aunt Addie's theory of learning:

9

I tell you one thing, if you learn it by yourself, if you have to get down and dig for it, it never leaves you. It stays here as long as you live because you had to dig it out of the mud before you learned it. (Norton in Wigginton, 1985, introduction)

The main proposition of constructivism is that learning means *constructing*, creating, inventing, and developing our own knowledge. Others can give us information, we can find information in books, and we can get information from the media, but as important as information is—and it is very important—receiving it, getting it, and hearing it does not necessarily equal learning. Learning in constructivist terms is

- both the process and the result of questioning, interpreting, and analyzing information;
- using this information and thinking process to develop, build, and alter our meaning and understanding of concepts and ideas; and
- integrating current experiences with our past experiences and what we already know about a given subject.

Each of us constructs our own meaning and learning about issues, problems, and topics. Because none of us has had exactly the same experiences as any other person, our understandings, our interpretations, and our schemata (knowledge constructs, learning) of any concept cannot be exactly the same as anyone else's. Our prior experiences, knowledge, and learning affect how we interpret and experience new events; our interpretations, in turn, affect construction of our knowledge structures and define our new learning.

Let's assume students are reading a story about a cat. Each student comes to class with a different understanding of the concept "cat." One student might be thinking cats are warm and cuddly; another might be thinking about how a cat's scratch can hurt. Given the meaning and past experiences each student has in relation to cats, the story itself takes on a different understanding for each student. Or, think about the day you were teaching about the causes of the Civil War or the seasons of the year or. . . . How many of your students really got it? How do you know how many got it? How many got it in the same way you meant it? Half of the students? Three quarters of the students? One student?

It is because we all make our own meanings and understandings of issues, concepts, and problems that the emphasis in a constructivist classroom is not on transmitting information but on promoting learning through student intellectual activity such as questioning, investigating, problem generating, and problem solving. It's about constructing knowledge, not receiving it.

It's About Thinking and Analyzing (Crap Detecting), Not Accumulating and Memorizing Information

Frankly, I'm bored out of my gourd with it [traditional classroom teaching]. . . . The essence of learning is the reading and research and application and what we've turned it into in the public schools is memory. (White in Page, 1992)

Constructivism is about thinking and the thinking process rather than about the quantity of information a student can memorize and recite, or in the case of math for example, about answers based on memorized formulas. This does not mean that content is not important. On the contrary, content is very important; however, in a constructivist classroom, a teacher does not stand and deliver most or even much of the content material. Rather, students uncover, discover, and reflect on content and their conceptions of such through inquiry, investigation, research, and analysis in the context of a problem, critical question, issue, or theme. Students gain and are encouraged to develop through these processes the ability to think for themselves, and to think critically; that is, to discriminate between the relevant and the irrelevant, to look at issues from different perspectives, to interpret and analyze written and electronic data, and, as some famous people—including George Plimpton (graduation speech, 1989), Postman and Weingartner (1969, p. 3), Ernest Hemingway, and songwriter Paul Simon in his song Kodachrome (1973)—would put it, *to "detect crap."*

It's About Understanding and Applying, Not Repeating Back

Constructivism focuses on in-depth understanding, not regurgitating and repeating back.

> With the traditional education we're doing, people remember . . .
> 10% of what they learn. . . . They don't remember anything after
> the final exam anyway. . . . (White, quoted in Page, 1992)

Although some teachers call traditional education methods efficient
in that they (the teachers) can transmit much material to students in
a short amount of time, they do not consider how ineffective this
delivery is in terms of students' understanding, retention, and application. How do you know if students *understand* concepts, issues,
ideas, and problems? If a student repeats information, as often happens in a traditional class, it doesn't mean she understands anything
or can apply this information in any way; it doesn't demonstrate
learning or understanding—it simply demonstrates ability to repeat
information. In a constructivist classroom, students demonstrate
their learning and understanding through various means. They
might develop new critical questions, they might write a script for a
video, they might summarize key ideas in their own words, they
might produce or create something, and/or they might frame and
solve problems.

It's About Being Active, Not Passive

> There is no such thing as genuine knowledge and fruitful under-
> standing except as offspring of doing. (Dewey, 1916, p. 321)

Although information is important, passively accumulating disconnected information is not learning. Passively receiving ready-
made knowledge from someone or something else is not learning. To
learn, a student has to be mentally and often physically active. A
student learns (that is, builds knowledge structures) when she discovers her own answers, solutions, concepts, and relationships and
creates her own interpretations. Although constructivists differ on
details of the concept of learning, all propose that when students
conduct their own learning, discover their own answers, and create
their own interpretations, their learning is deeper, more comprehensive, and longer lasting, and the learning that occurs actively leads
to an ability to think critically (Dewey, 1933; Freire, 1981; Kilpatrick,
1918, 1929; Sharan & Sharan, 1989/1990; Wigginton, 1989). They also
all agree that learning is *not* what Goodlad (1984) described in his
study of schooling. Learning is *not*

a lot of teacher talk and a lot of student listening . . . ; almost invariably closed and factual questions; little corrective feedback and not guidance; and predominantly total class instructional configuration around traditional activities—all in a virtually affectless environment. (p. 242)

It also is *not* what a high school student described:

I don't do a lot in school. . . . I don't like any of the high school classes really. You just sit there and they tell you something and they give you a test and you tell it right back to them. Everybody has the same answer on the test if you do it right. (Clark in Page, 1992)

What's New Is Really Old: Or, Looking Back to the Future

Rejection of Traditional Education

Traditional education is "guaranteed to rot your brain" (Commager, 1980, p. 34). One of the themes that all proponents of constructivism (active learning) have in common is the rejection of the traditional teacher-dominated classroom in which the teacher manages, controls, and dispenses the information (Page, 1990). They see this education not only as passive and controlling but also dysfunctional in relation to individual, democratic, and societal needs. They see it as stifling students' creativity, autonomy, independent thinking, competence, confidence, and self-esteem and as making students dependent, conforming, and nonthinking. The historical connections and progressions allow us to make sense of constructivism today and to understand where Susan got some of her ideas. Let's take a look at how some well-known educators, philosophers, and psychologists felt and feel about traditional education.

Rousseau and Pestalozzi

Jean-Jacques Rousseau (1762/1957) lived during the age known as the Enlightenment and is thought by many to have inspired the French Revolution with his stinging essays on society and government.

He believed that the classical education of his time, which consisted of reading and memorizing, prevented students from being active, which in turn caused them to be passive, destructive, deceitful, selfish, and stupid. He argued that this education was boring and beyond the child's comprehension, and that it taught students "to believe much and know little" (p. 90). Johann Heinrich Pestalozzi (1801/1898), a disciple of Rousseau, devoted much of his life to teaching the orphans of the French Revolution. Like Rousseau, Pestalozzi claimed that this classical education, which was "blown in their ears" (p. 244), made students anxious, confused, and passive. He noted that students memorized information but did not understand.

Dewey and Kilpatrick

When John Dewey opened his laboratory school in Chicago in 1896, American education was essentially the classical education of Pestalozzi's time and similar to that Dewey himself had experienced as boring (Campbell, 1971). Dewey objected to the content and method of this classical education because it did not involve problem solving or reflective thinking. Instead, students memorized and recited unrelated chunks of material (Dewey, 1931/1970) and became docile (Dewey, 1938/1972). William Heard Kilpatrick, a graduate student of Dewey, claimed that the inflexibility of traditional room set-ups and of the traditional teacher-student relationship squelched natural ability and led to passive and unintelligent conformity (Connell, 1980; Kilpatrick, 1929). He argued that teachers were concerned mainly with students being able to recite material without error (Tyler, 1975).

Piaget and Bruner

Jean Piaget, a Swiss biologist and psychologist interested in how humans adapted to the environment, met several times with American educators—including John Dewey—during the 1920s and 1930s. He expanded on Dewey's argument against traditional education with his claim that the traditional instructional method of teacher telling students required that the teacher and student (listener) have mutual communication frameworks, but that that was not realistic. He argued that a student heard what he perceived and that that might not be the same thing as what the teacher was saying. What teachers taught, therefore, was not always what the students learned (Labinowicz, 1980; Piaget, 1941/1995).

Jerome Bruner, a psychologist, met and worked with Piaget and also was one of the group of American scholars, educators, and scientists who, during the late 1950s and early 1960s, were rewriting math, science, and social studies curricula as a result of the educational debate that occurred after the launching of Sputnik. (They called it the "new science," the "new math," and the "new social studies.") Like those already mentioned, Bruner rejects the teacher-as-knowledge-dispenser model of traditional education (Bruner, 1961). He claims, as did Dewey and Kilpatrick, that the teaching of information out of context results in rote nonsense because the delivered content is not connected to or associated with student action, and students do not form the necessary cognitive connections to understand the material (Bruner, 1971).

Freire, Wigginton, and Sharan

Paulo Freire, a South American scholar and revolutionary, described traditional education as involving a vertical relationship in which teachers are on top, students are on the bottom, and there is no room for student dialogue. He saw traditional education as working *on* a student rather than with him. As did Rousseau, Pestalozzi, Dewey, and Kilpatrick before him, Freire (1981) asserted that this education has no place for original thought and forces students to conform to the existing social system (Freire, 1974). Freire (1974) called this the banking model of education. In this model, the teacher (the banker) makes deposits into the depositories (the students). They receive and file the deposits, and that is that.

Eliot Wigginton and Shlomo Sharan are two contemporary educators with similar messages. Wigginton (1985), founder of the *Fox-fire* program for teaching English, describes students in a traditional classroom setting as bored receivers who are glued to lectures, textbooks, and memorizing. The teacher is the boss and has all the knowledge. The result is rebellious and alienated students. (What was it Rousseau said about students becoming destructive?)

Not as well known, but with a similar message, is Shlomo Sharan, a professor at Tel Aviv University and developer of the cooperative learning program called Group Investigation. Like Bruner, Sharan

(Sharan, 1985) claims that the traditional teaching model, in which the teacher dominates and transmits knowledge and the student is passive, does not allow the student to process information and therefore does not lead to any meaning or comprehension for the student.

Constructivist Learning Theories

Active learning is guaranteed to expand the brain. Just as these educators, philosophers, and psychologists agree and agreed on what doesn't work, they agree and agreed on what does. Although they expressed or may express their theories of learning in different terms, the theories revolve around the same propositions.

- Students learn more when they are actively engaged in their own learning.
- By investigating and discovering for themselves, by creating and re-creating, and by interacting with the environment, students build their own knowledge structures.
- Learning actively leads to an ability to think critically and to solve problems.
- Through an active learning approach, students learn content and process at the same time (Page, 1990).

Although not all these educators, psychologists, and philosophers necessarily would have used or would use the word *constructivist* to describe themselves, the core concept of their theories of learning was and is that students construct their own knowledge when they are mentally active in or on their environment.

Rousseau and Pestalozzi

Rousseau's *Emile* (1762/1957), his treatise on what education should be, is often considered the foundation of progressivism (Sahakian & Sahakian, 1974) or of what today we would call constructivism. Rousseau (1762/1957) believed that students learn through their senses, experience, and activity. Through the senses, the child discovers, compares, and judges what he experiences, and what results are impressions called ideas. Reasoning, Rousseau asserted, is the act of sorting, associating, connecting, and discriminating among and between these simple ideas to form complex ideas and relationships. It is the child's interaction with the environment—his experiences—that correct and modify these ideas. For Rousseau, the core concept of learning would be a compound of ideas.

Similarly, Pestalozzi (1801/1898) believed that the student's mind receives impressions through observation and experience and that these impressions produce ideas and an organized mental structure that enables the student to compare, examine, separate, sort, and conclude. He used the term *anschauung* (p. 7) to refer to the mental process through which the ideas and mental structures are developed. He claimed this process by which people form concepts and ideas was the source of all human cognition.

Dewey and Kilpatrick

For Dewey, the central idea was intellectual integration. He described (1931/1970) the mind in a mentally active student as "roaming far and wide" (p. 34) but returning with what it found and constantly making judgments as to relationships, relevancies, and bearings upon a central theme. This process of integration included seeking, finding, using, organizing, digesting, and assimilating information. Like Rousseau and Pestalozzi, Dewey (1933, 1938/1972) talked about the interaction between the learner and the environment. His theory was that what one learned in one situation helped to direct the understanding and action of future situations. This person/environment interaction led to a continual reconstruction of impulses and thought. Dewey described the mind as a verb, as something to do rather than something to be filled like a sponge. He believed that because students need to interact with their environment in order to think, every student should be engaged in activity around a project (Dewey, 1933; Ernst, 1953). For projects to be educative, Dewey (1933) argued, they needed to fit the student's interest, involve the student actively, have intrinsic worth, present problems that would lead to new questions and inquiry, and involve a considerable time span.

Dewey's student Kilpatrick similarly asserted that thinking is the intelligent, interactive adaptation between the person and the environment (Kilpatrick, 1933/1969). Although Kilpatrick's idea of project work involved more student autonomy than did Dewey's, Kilpatrick, like Dewey, believed that projects should be the center of the curriculum because they would increase student motivation and involvement, turn boring schoolwork into meaningful activity, and at the same time increase student knowledge and skill.

Piaget and Bruner

One cannot overestimate Piaget's contributions to the direction, meaning, and understanding of contemporary constructivism. Here we present two of his most important ideas about how people learn. First, we get the term *schemata*, which refers to knowledge structures/constructs and ways of perceiving, understanding, and thinking about the world, from Piaget. According to Piaget, learners construct their own knowledge schemes in relation to, and filtered through, previous and current experiences. Second, Piaget described mental development (learning) as a process of equilibrium in response to external stimuli. That is, in the interaction with the environment, he theorized, the student assimilates complementary components of the external world into his existing cognitive structures (schemata); if new experiences do not fit the existing knowledge structures or schemes, the student will change or alter those structures to accommodate the new information. The processes of assimilation and accommodation create equilibrium (Piaget, 1967/1971; Weil & Murphy, 1982). When an external disturbance causes disequilibrium, he believed, the student has to think in order to resolve the conflict. The process of maintaining equilibrium—construction and reconstruction of knowledge—in relation to the environment is what creates cognitive growth (Piaget, 1967/1971; Labinowicz, 1980). For knowledge to be meaningful, students need to construct it themselves.

Discovery is the core of Bruner's theory. Whatever a person discovers for himself is what he truly knows. From discovery, Bruner asserts, comes increased intellectual ability, including the ability to solve problems. This discovery is a matter of students thinking about and rearranging material in terms of their interests and cognitive structures (Bruner's phrase for schemata) in a way that leads to new insights and new inquiry. The goal is for students to be autonomous and self-propelled thinkers (Bruner, 1961).

Freire and Wigginton

For Freire, education should involve a critical dialogue and an active search for knowledge that leads to positive action in society. Students need to inquire, to create and re-create, and to participate actively in their own learning. When interacting with the environment, Freire (1981) asserted, the student discovers and mentally organizes knowledge. This knowledge or learning becomes the basis for knowledge that will replace it. Freire, like Dewey, believed that gaining knowledge requires constant searching and that the only person who learns is the one who invents and re-invents his learning and then uses it in concrete situations. He called this mentally organized knowledge.

Wigginton's (1989) theory, similar to many of the others, is that what the student learns and figures out for himself is what he knows. Actions leading to discoveries are internalized (cognitive processes) and remembered. Projects, he believes—similarly to Rousseau, Pestalozzi, Dewey, and Kilpatrick—should flow from the student's own interests, reflections, and evaluations; and problem solving, as advocated by Dewey, should not be an end in itself but should lead to other questions and problems.

Sharan

Sharan (1985) believes that students learn best through problem solving. Topics and methods of learning become personally relevant to the students when they engage in the process of investigation typical of a particular discipline or profession—that is, in a science class, the students work as scientists; in a history class, students work as historians. Like Dewey and Piaget, Sharan believes that through active learning the student organizes and assimilates the experience and that this process helps the student to develop logical thought and higher-order thinking skills. He believes that students understand events in relation to their past experiences and level of development.

Research Results

Past and contemporary research results on the use of active learning methods associated with the tenets of constructivism are overwhelmingly positive. The greatest difference between the older research and the newest research is in the sophistication of the contemporary research tools and methods. The research as a whole shows active learning methods to be superior to teacher-dominated approaches in measures of academic, affective, and skill learning.

Looking Back (The First Half of the 20th Century)

In a study of the project method, research demonstrated that students at the Winnetka Schools (Washburne & Raths, 1927), who worked on projects during the first half of the day and on individualized subject matter during the second half, were better prepared than those from three other towns of similar social composition. The Winnetka students, who joined the students of the three other towns in a regional high school, were the only ones who scored above average on all major subject tests.

The most extensive research study of active learning methods and results began in 1933. The Progressive Education Association conducted this Eight Year Study, which involved 30 high schools implementing progressive innovations. All the schools used activities and methods based on the active learning tenets discussed above. Three hundred colleges agreed to eliminate standard entrance requirements for graduates of these high schools and to accept the students on the basis of their interest and their ability to work successfully as determined by the high school (Greene, 1942). The researchers matched 1,475 of the original 2,000 progressive students with graduates of conventional schools in terms of scholastic aptitude, interests, and socioeconomic background. The first follow-up began in 1936 as the first graduates entered college. Researchers added a new graduating class each year until 1939. Based on these students' college records, instructors' reports, written work, and student questionnaires and interviews, the authors concluded that graduates of the progressive schools were "on the whole" (Aiken, 1942, p. 149) more successful than their matches and that students whose high school programs were most different from traditional programs were much superior to their traditional school counterparts (Aiken, 1942; Darling-Hammond, 1993; Greene, 1942; Walten & Travers, 1963).

More Recently (1950-Present)

Several contemporary (depending on your age and how you define this term) comparative studies have focused on results of active learning approaches. In a comparative study of two learning methods, Phillips and Faris (1977) concluded that students probably will learn more if given the chance to do so in nontraditional ways. In their study of two groups of senior government students, one group worked in the traditional lecture and discussion mode; the other group used innovative and active learning techniques including independent study and internships. The active learning students surpassed the traditional students in achievement after the first few weeks. In another comparative study that measured retention of 8th and 9th graders after a geography field trip, MacKenzie and White (1982) found that students who had acquired and processed their own information on the field trip showed marked superiority in retention of knowledge over the field-trip students who were given information by the teacher.

A 6-week study by Worthen (1968) involved 423 5th- and 6th-grade math students, half learning with a discovery method and the other half being taught by direct instruction. This study showed the direct instruction method to be superior on initial recall but the discovery method to be superior on retention and transfer. In a study by Kersh (1962) of 90 high school students studying two rules of addition, data supported the hypothesis that self-discovery motivates the student to practice more and thus to remember and transfer more than does direct teaching.

For several studies (Massialas & Zevin, 1967) involving different social studies classes in two Chicago high schools over a 3-year period, teachers developed and used new discovery materials and approaches. Analysis of interview data showed that with discovery approaches

- there was a greater exchange of ideas between students;
- student participation doubled;
- students learned how to organize and form hypotheses and to use, interpret, and apply evidence; and
- students looked at knowledge as tentative rather than absolute.

Finally, in a meta-review of the effectiveness of process-oriented science programs, involving 57 studies, Bredderman (1983) found significant gains in creativity, intelligence, language use, and math.

And There's More

The Sudbury Valley School in Framingham, Massachusetts, is a K-12 school with no entrance or learning requirements. The school supports student-directed activities and offers courses only when students show interest. There are no grades and no evaluations. To graduate, the student has to defend a thesis at a meeting of the school's Assembly and has to prove he is ready to take responsibility for himself. Gray and Chanoff (1986) conducted a follow-up study of 78 graduates. At the time these graduates had entered the Sudbury School, more than one-third of them had had serious school problems including truancy, rebellion, learning disabilities, anxiety, and emotional disturbances. The authors surveyed the graduates using questionnaires, telephone contact, and personal interviews. The data revealed that there were no apparent difficulties being admitted to college and that the graduates were successful in a wide range of careers. Students reported that the school had helped them develop their own interests and responsibility as well as to develop initiative, curiosity, the ability to communicate with all people, and an appreciation of democratic values.

And More

Cooperative learning methods are not necessarily constructivist. Some cooperative learning methods involve a teacher-dominated method (Slavin, 1989) and are concerned with the learning of basic skills involving right and wrong answers. Sharan's (1985) Group Investigation method, however, focuses on higher level learning. The objectives of Group Investigation programs are to get students actively involved in their own learning and for students to learn a critical thinking process; students control the goals, learning is student-directed, and the rewards are intrinsic. In the Group Investigation model, students work in small groups and gather, analyze, and evaluate data and draw conclusions on a topic of their choosing. They then prepare a report and presentation for the class. Peers and teachers evaluate the work (Sharan & Sharan, 1976, 1989/1990).

In five large-scale comparative studies of the Group Investigation method, Sharan and Sharan (1989/1990) found that Group Investigation students in elementary and secondary schools had a higher level of academic achievement than the students in traditional classes. The Group Investigation students also did better on questions assessing higher-level learning, although sometimes only just as well on acquiring information. On tests of social interaction, the traditional teaching methods stimulated a great deal of competition among students, whereas the Group Investigation method promoted cooperation, mutual assistance, and social interaction among classmates from different ethnic groups. A more recent study of Group Investigation (Sharan & Shachar, 1988) involved 8th grade classes in Israel. Four classes used traditional teaching methods, and four used the Group Investigation method. Teachers were assigned at random and participated in a series of training workshops during the pilot part of the study. During the actual experiment, there were 197 students in the Group Investigation and 154 in the traditional group. Results based on pre- and posttests, student-prepared discussions, and videotapes showed a highly superior level of achievement in the Group Investigation classes as compared to the traditional classes in both high- and lower-level thinking.

And More

In a 2-year study of secondary world history students, Booth (1980) found that students made significant gains in their abstract thinking abilities and concluded that the improvement was the result of an active learning approach (including investigation and interpretation of primary sources), not innate student development. Goodlad (1984) found that students rated history as one of their least favorite and one of the least interesting courses. Other research shows that this negative attitude and lack of interest is more a reflection of teaching method than of subject matter. For example, Shemilt (1980) found that students in an active learning, in-depth, primary-source-based course in history were less likely to find history boring than students in traditional classes. Furthermore, Newmann (in Jenness, 1990) found, after observing social studies teachers over a substantial time in different areas, that the classes involving more in-depth study and research of topics had fewer bored students than traditional classes.

Still More

Two large qualitative studies also support active learning processes. A study (Page, 1992) of the National History Day Program, a grade 5-12 program grounded in active learning propositions, showed that the participating students developed their own conclusions and their own knowledge. Additionally, the students expressed a deeper awareness of issues involved in the topics they were researching and believed that they learned content better, had higher comprehension, and obtained transferable skills to a greater degree than possible in a traditional classroom. Puckett's study (1986) of *Foxfire*, a program in which students create articles, books, videotapes, and radio shows on life in Appalachia as a way to learn English, showed similar results. Puckett found that compared to the boring and ineffective education described in books by Goodlad (1984) and by Sizer (1984), *Foxfire*'s accomplishments have been extraordinary, especially in its community/school relationships and in providing students with the opportunity to make decisions and to conduct their own learning.

And Finally

In 1993, researchers from Vanderbilt University; the University of California, Berkeley; and the Ontario Institute for Studies in Education developed a project called Schools for Thought. The underlying foundation for this project is the belief that students construct their own knowledge. Classrooms in the Schools for Thought program focus on students developing critical thinking skills, such as acquiring and analyzing information through inquiry and investigation, and on student communication of findings to authentic adult audiences. The main principles of the program include

1. student choice of research topics within a teacher-determined and core content framework;
2. group work;
3. individual student accountability;
4. integration of process and content;
5. creation of authentic products and involvement of authentic audiences such as community members; and
6. authentic use of technology.

In a study comparing student achievement in a 6th grade Schools for Thought program in Nashville to student achievement in other classrooms, researchers found that on "10 subtests of the TCAP [Tennessee Comprehensive Assessment Program] . . . students scored as well as, or significantly better than, the comparison classes on all of the subtests" (Secules, Cottom, Bray, & Miller, 1997, p. 58). On a complex performance assessment that measured high-level critical thinking skills, Schools for Thought students "scored significantly higher" (p. 58) than students in other classrooms (Secules et al., 1997).

The research base is clear and growing: Active learning programs in which students construct their own knowledge lead to the development of critical and independent thinking skills, deeper understanding of concepts, and longer-lasting learning. We can't ignore these findings.

> Dewey's ideas are alive and well in our own post-industrial times. . . . One thing is new, advocates argue: ideas that in the past were supported merely by the armchair theorizing of influential philosophers today are grounded in empirical evidence. (Donmoyer, 1996, p. 4)

Although this research provides support for anyone wanting to implement constructivist activities in his or her classroom, in the long run what matters are *your* findings, *your* results, *your* observations, and *your* experiences. If you and your students can develop successful active learning programs and experience positive results connected to your efforts, that is the real test.

Do We Have to Know This for the Test?

In 1978, the National Science Foundation released a seven-volume report on the status of math, science, and social studies education (Puckett, 1986). This report found that the "dominant mode of instruction [continued] to be large group, teacher-controlled recitation and lecture, based primarily on the textbook" (Shaver, Davis, & Helburn, in Puckett, 1986, p. 390). Those results are basically the same as the results from three studies in the 1980s by Goodlad (1984), Boyer (1983), and Sizer (1984) that concluded that "classroom practice is largely devoid of student inquiry, discovery learning, and other innovative strategies" (Puckett, 1986, p. 389). When Cuban (1983) examined changes since 1870 in theory, curriculum, and resources in relation to classroom instruction, he found that although theories, philosophies, textbooks, and curricula had changed, there was little evidence of change in teacher practice and that teacher-dominated instruction was remarkably stable at all levels of schooling even though reformers have and had been fighting against teacher-dominated instruction since the mid-1850s (Cuban, 1990).

Furthermore, since the early 1980s there has been an avalanche of literature on the need for reform in schools. Much of that rhetoric refers to the inappropriateness and ineffectiveness of this teacher-dominated teaching method in an age when torrents and explosions of information require that students learn how to find, select, organize, interpret, and use that information. When Boyer (1988) studied the impact of the Sizer (1984), Boyer (1983), and Goodlad (1984) research and of the school reform that followed, he found some progress but suggested that

> the focus continues to be on memorization and recall. Textbooks still control curriculum in the nation's schools. . . . Also, there is great passivity in the classroom where often the most frequent question asked is: "Do we have to know this for the test?" (p. 5)

His prescription is as follows:

> If students are to excel, they must be engaged actively in learning. The mastery of subject matter is essential. But unless students are creative, independent thinkers, unless they acquire the tools and motivation to go on learning, [the] prospect for excellence will be enormously diminished. (p. 5)

We can call it experiential, discovery, or student-centered learning; we can call it the project method; we can call it democratic education or learning by doing; we can call it situated or anchored cognition. These all refer to and promote the same thing—students developing their own knowledge and improved student achievement.

The Best Part: Moving This to Your Classroom

Why Now?

We can go back to Rousseau, to the ancient Greeks, or even to prehistoric man to find a rationale for active learning approaches, but if Cuban (1990) found little change in teacher-dominated methods in the last 100 years, how can we expect it to happen now? We might expect change for two reasons: because we are in "one of those rare periods in history when large numbers of people are receptive to major changes in education" (Goldman in Prawat, 1992, p. 354) and because our need for such approaches is more urgent now than ever. A teacher-dominated instructional system that delivers information cannot work in an age of information explosion. Estimates 10 years ago (Hartoonian, 1984) were that information would increase 100% every 24 months. The estimate now is that it is increasing 100% every 6 months. The student who passively receives information has no notion of what it means to be a responsible citizen in a democratic society or a worker who needs to take initiative and responsibility. To paraphrase Piaget (in Labinowicz, 1980), if it takes one of your students 3 years to discover and create her own knowledge about several topics and it takes you only 1 month to deliver information on the same subjects, you have just wasted 1 month. Do you want to waste more time?

Debunking the Myths

Changing your classroom from a traditional one to a constructivist one will not happen overnight. It is a progressive process that requires doing and reflecting, more doing and reflecting, and then more doing and reflecting. You may in fact have first experiences similar to Susan's. The key to successful efforts, in addition to your ongoing reflection and persistence, is in your clear understanding of the constructivist concepts and what those concepts look like when applied in a classroom. Following is a list of statements made either by students in our Learning Theory classes or by teachers with whom we have worked who are involved in making changes in their classrooms. Let's take a look at where your current understanding of constructivism is. Remember that constructivism is a theory about how people learn. It is a theory that says that learning means constructing and developing one's own knowledge; that we do this by actively questioning, interpreting, problem solving, and creating; and that in-depth understanding is one result of this learning. Take the challenge. Mark off the statements with which you agree.

Challenge Statements

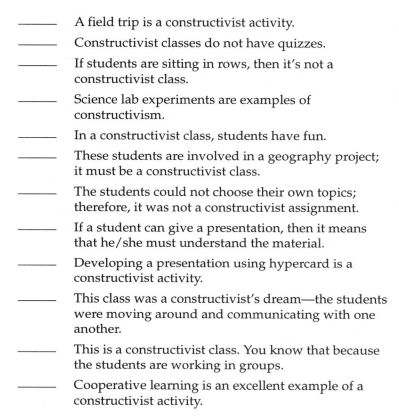

——— A field trip is a constructivist activity.

——— Constructivist classes do not have quizzes.

——— If students are sitting in rows, then it's not a constructivist class.

——— Science lab experiments are examples of constructivism.

——— In a constructivist class, students have fun.

——— These students are involved in a geography project; it must be a constructivist class.

——— The students could not choose their own topics; therefore, it was not a constructivist assignment.

——— If a student can give a presentation, then it means that he/she must understand the material.

——— Developing a presentation using hypercard is a constructivist activity.

——— This class was a constructivist's dream—the students were moving around and communicating with one another.

——— This is a constructivist class. You know that because the students are working in groups.

——— Cooperative learning is an excellent example of a constructivist activity.

How many statements did you agree with, and which ones were they? Remember again that constructivism is a theory about how people learn. Review the statements using this as a frame of reference. Do you still agree with the same statements? Give yourself one point for each statement with which you agreed.

If you scored between 9 and 12, don't waste another minute; read and study the rest of this book as quickly as possible.

If you scored between 4 and 8, categorize the statements you agreed with by issues and look at the chapters that address these issues.

If you scored 3 or less, and it is because you feel there isn't enough information in any of the statements to clarify and define learning, *please* don't leave education. Students need you.

Why does a high score suggest the need for more study of the tenets of constructivism?

The answer is that there is not enough information in *any* of these statements to allow you to determine whether the statement is valid. For example, if the field trip is teacher-directed and students are simply filling in blanks on a worksheet without investigating, discovering, and problem solving, it would not be constructivist. Likewise, just because students are working in groups, it does not mean they are involved in a constructivist activity. We would have to know more about the purpose and context of the activity and also about the kind of student-to-student communication and interaction that was or was not occurring in the groups.

We suggest that you revisit the statements above often as you work your way through the book and as you become more familiar with what constructivism looks like in a classroom.

The Road Map

How will creating a constructivist classroom affect you and your students? Ultimately, if you take your time and reflect and act appropriately on results, student learning and your place and role in the classroom can change drastically for the better. There is no one way to create a constructivist classroom, and, as you have seen from Susan's story, there are no guarantees. Constructivist classrooms don't all look or work the same way. Like life, this is more of a journey than a destination. If you are ready to start the journey, read on . . .

Three

Coming of Age

The Active Learning Movement

Our journey in this chapter starts with a look at similarities between past and contemporary reform movements and how the contemporary movements in the K-4, 5-8, and 9-12 grades are connected to constructivist propositions. Add to this foundation an overview of the new standards of the major professional teacher organizations and you will be ready to move along to look at Your Own Classroom in the next chapter.

From the Activity Movement
to the Active Learning Movements

After reading in Chapter 2 about what philosophers, psychologists, and educators over the last 200 years have seen as *ineffective* in terms of student learning, the following should sound familiar:

> Educators reject classical education and expository teaching, competition between students for grades, the use of memory and rote learning, and the domination of the class by the teacher. They support student initiated experiences, experiments, problem solving, the scientific method, long term projects, cooperative planning, the interrelatedness and integration of subject matter and democracy in action in the classroom. (Page, 1990, p. 48)

The educators referred to here were the progressive educators of the early 1900s, and these viewpoints were the foundation of the Progressive Education Movement of the same time period.

A Word of Warning

If these ideas sound familiar in another context, it is because they are also the core of the contemporary reform movements; as a whole, we will call these new movements the Active Learning Movement. As with the Progressive Education Movement of the early 20th century, there are many misinterpretations of what these propositions should look like when translated into action in the classroom, and there are different groups within the movement who simply view them differently. In the Progressive Education Movement, there was a child-centered faction that focused on extreme individual freedom, self-expression, individual initiative, and curriculum (Connell, 1980). Dewey and Kilpatrick were opposed to this child-centered direction of progressive education. As Dewey explained,

> There is a present tendency in so-called schools of educational thought . . . to say in effect, let us surround pupils with materials, tools, appliances etc., and let pupils respond according to their own desires. Above all, let us not suggest any end or plan to the students; let us not suggest to them what they shall do, for that is unwarranted trespass upon their sacred intellectual individuality since the essence of such individuality is to set up ends and means. Now such a method is really stupid for it attempts the impossible, which is always stupid, and it misconceives the conditions of independent thinking. (Dewey in Rusk, 1956, p. 106)

Like Dewey, we see total child-centered permissiveness and complete student-directed activity without teacher guidance, in most cases, as nonsense. Pre-service teachers who try to implement constructivist models in the classroom, however, often make the unfounded leap from traditional formats to total student and classroom freedom, which almost always spells chaos—and little learning—in the classroom. We will deal more with this idea later in several sections, but we want to be clear at the outset that we do not advocate this kind of hands-off approach to student learning, nor do we believe that current reform movements support such an approach.

Teachers cannot be inactive bystanders to student activity and learning; they have to redefine, however, what it is they can and should do to allow and encourage responsible student initiative for optimum learning.

The Activity Movement

The Activity Movement (part of the Progressive Education Movement) of the early 1900s evolved from Kilpatrick's project method. The premise of this movement was that acquiring and developing knowledge should be an active (mental and physical) process that should involve a project. Keep in mind that this did not mean students could or should do whatever they felt like or wanted to do. The movement stressed that

- The interests and needs of the student should determine the nature of the project.
- There should be enough different kinds of projects to allow all students to succeed.
- The work should be cooperative.
- School organization should be democratic.

The Activity Movement became so large that in 1934 the National Society for the Study of Education devoted an entire volume of its *33rd Yearbook* to its study. The study reported the following positive aspects of the activity method.

- It improves students' abilities to think, plan, and do.
- It develops initiative.
- It leads to better understanding of life.
- It creates new student/teacher relationships.
- It provides motivation.
- It increases the students' interest in school.
- It leads students to read more.
- It allows for more self-expression.
- It leads to standards of achievement in subject areas as high or higher than in a traditional method.

Contemporary Active Learning Movements

This far into the book, you probably are aware that constructivist ideas do not simply represent the theoretical musings of disgruntled education professors. Instead, although "how to" books are rare, constructivism not only has a long distinguished history but also has truly come of age. About 30 years ago, practical, teacher-friendly incarnations of constructivist ideas began to crop up in schools all across the country. Although some of these models withered on the vine, other approaches, once thought to be radical, have begun to take hold because they have proved so useful in facilitating *learning*. In the next section, we will examine some of the major reform efforts that have taken hold at the elementary, middle, and secondary levels.

Say Good-bye to Dick and Jane: The Whole Language Movement

Reform at the Elementary Level

The Whole Language Movement, perhaps more than any other reform movement at the elementary level, has significantly changed what classroom teachers actually do. Whole language is at once both theoretical and prescriptive. It describes a particular set of beliefs about the ways in which children learn to read, and it advocates a distinct approach to the teaching of reading. What are these beliefs? What do whole language proponents suggest elementary classroom teachers do? How is this connected to constructivism? Let's begin by reviewing the fundamentals.

First and foremost, whole language approaches emphasize that a child's experiences, interests, and needs should be central to the reading curriculum. As noted in Chapter 2, new learning takes place when students integrate new information with what they already know (as Dewey would say, new skills and information become part of a "continuum of learning"). This is why whole language approaches advocate learner-centered curricula: If the world of text is to be useful and appealing—in short, if it is to facilitate learning—it must connect with the world of the child (MacInnis & Hemming, 1995). For this reason, whole language classrooms allow children to make greater choices in what they read and write about and, in general, the children take the lead as they pursue their own natural curiosities.

Whole language is learner-centered in a more fundamental way as well. Whole language proponents view reading, like spoken language, as a developmental process that unfolds gradually and naturally as it is nurtured by teachers; practiced in shared, social environments; and reinforced by positive role models in literature-rich settings. This means that teachers do less correcting and more modeling, just as parents do with their toddlers as they first begin to develop oral language.

Whole language emphasizes meaning and comprehension; skill development comes later, as a natural progression from this starting point. Traditional methods of teaching reading, on the other hand, begin with the building blocks—letters, sounds, sound/symbol relationships, and phonetic decoding skills—which, once mastered, can be put together by students to derive information and meaning from text. Instead of viewing reading instruction, in this way, as a highly structured, sequential presentation of specific skills, whole language advocates believe reading emerges when students are given the opportunity to discover generalizations about spelling, grammar, and syntactic patterns.

Children in whole language classrooms are also encouraged to write as early as possible; as they do, they are forced to pay attention to the ways in which letters represent sounds in consistent phonemic patterns. This whole language approach is often referred to as "invented spelling" because teachers typically and initially refrain from correcting spelling errors and use a child's written production as a measure of his/her mastery of the sound/symbol relationship.

The "whole" in "whole language" also refers to the use of what has been called authentic children's literature. Unlike basal readers like the old *Dick and Jane* series, which are contrived and frequently contain controlled vocabularies, real stories, songs, and poems, like *I Know an Old Lady Who Swallowed a Fly*, contain predictable patterns and rhythms of natural language that are acquired by children after repeated exposure and appropriate modeling. Children also create their *own* reading material in whole language settings by dictating stories to teachers. The teachers transcribe the stories, which the students can read and re-read.

There are other fundamental differences between the *Dick and Jane* approach and the *I Know an Old Lady* approach. Some of these are summarized in Table 3.1. Should teachers teach specific subskills like phonics directly, or should we allow children to discover sound/

TABLE 3.1 Differences in Approaches to Reading

The *Here Come Dick and Jane* Approach	The *I Know an Old Lady Who Swallowed a Fly* (Whole Language) Approach
Uses basal readers, which often have a controlled vocabulary, as beginning reading material.	Uses children's "authentic" literature as well as a child's own language as beginning reading material.
Treats reading, writing, and oral language as separate subjects—may even *teach* these during separate parts of the day.	Sees reading, writing, and oral language as interwoven; students *learn* together in an integrated fashion.
Emphasizes sound/symbol relationship, long and short vowels, consonant blends, and other parts of language strongly emphasized and *teaches* them as individual skills, separate from the reading process.	Students *learn* phonics skills in context, as they discover patterns in words; students test hypotheses while engaged in the reading of literature.
Emphasizes skill development; students practice subskills using worksheets and drill.	Emphasizes meaning and comprehension; students practice by reading, writing, singing, and discussing.
Teacher typically selects materials.	Students typically select materials.
Views reading as a separate type of language development that should be *taught* sequentially.	Views reading in the context of language development that should be *learned* holistically.
Considers assessment, like *teaching* reading, in a piecemeal fashion and focuses on separate subskills (e.g., phonetic decoding, spelling, grammar, comprehension).	Considers assessment, like *learning* to read, holistically and focuses on miscue analysis and portfolio development.
Teaches spelling rules in isolation; teachers correct spelling errors and students practice spelling words in isolation until they reach mastery.	Teachers encourage writing as soon as children can hold a pencil or crayon, accept "invented spellings," and use the successive approximations as a measure of a child's evolution toward grasping the sound/symbol relationship.

symbol relationships more naturally as they read and write? The jury is still out; there is a significant body of evidence to support both points of view. Research has consistently shown, however, that as many as 1 in 5 students (Lyon, 1995; Shaywitz, 1995) may actually have a disability in the area of phonological awareness that prevents them from naturally acquiring sound/symbol relationships. These students require highly structured and systematic teacher-directed instruction in phonics. Even though some children appear better suited to a more traditional, phonics-based approach, all children benefit from classrooms that

- allow them to make choices about what they read;
- encourage them to make connections between what they read and what they know;
- integrate reading with meaningful content information;
- incorporate other language activities such as speaking, writing, and singing during reading activities; and
- make reading a playful and joyous activity.

Because whole language is not simply about reading but instead is also about writing, speaking, singing, and listening, many teachers, once introduced to this approach, have been inspired to make other fundamental changes in their classrooms. For example, Jan Carpenter, an elementary school teacher in Milton, Vermont, has used the whole language approach as a model for integrating many subject areas that she formerly taught as distinct academic disciplines. Music, art, and math may all be part of a science unit; scientific inquiry, mathematical calculation, and dance may become integral components of an American history unit. In Chapter 7, you will see how Jan Carpenter pulls disciplines together. Although integrating subject matter is not unique to the elementary level, this approach, like whole language, is an idea whose time has truly come of age for teachers who work in kindergarten to 4th-grade classrooms.

Dick and Jane Notice Each Other

Reform at the Middle Level

Because her mom wouldn't let her wear any makeup, Liz hid a big bag of it in her desk at school. Each morning, she set up a makeup mirror and decorated herself with gobs and gobs of color when she first got to her homeroom. At the end of the day, right before she got on the bus, the makeup came off. Then there was Mark Stratton, a quiet and handsome 7th grader. He came into school one morning in tears because kids on the bus had stuck gum in his hair. The gym teacher took care of him quickly—she got some scissors and gave Mark a crew cut. Welcome to life at the middle school.

Like contemporary emphasis on constructivist approaches to teaching and learning, middle school reform is not new. In 1893, the Committee of Ten, a subgroup of the national commission that the National Education Association sponsored to study the question of curriculum and schooling goals, recommended changes to the elementary/secondary configuration of schooling. Within the following 10 years, there were efforts to make schooling for students in the middle age groups something more than an elementary education and something other than a watered down version of high school. Although there were varied reasons for supporting a school in between the elementary grades and the high school—including speeding up the college preparation process and providing services to prevent dropping out (Brimm, 1963)—the basis of this new education in the middle was to be the young adolescents themselves: who they were, where they were in terms of mental and physical development, how they differed from elementary and high school students, and what they needed that was unique to their ages. There would be more in-depth curriculum than previously had been seen in the elementary schools and more of an emphasis on guidance, exploration, and responsibility (George, Stevenson, Thomason, & Beane, 1992). One of the main propositions of this change was consistent with contemporary constructivist propositions; that is, that an active learning and interdisciplinary approach should drive instruction and curriculum.

Although the majority of school systems had some form of a "school in the middle" by the 1960s, most of these were called junior high schools and, as the name implies, functioned as junior versions of the high schools. Largely because of political circumstances, including enrollment constraints (which forced districts to combine grades or schools), budgetary concerns, and parental demands, most junior high schools never implemented the recommended reforms in terms of structural organization, instruction, or curriculum.

The 1960s and 1970s saw renewed interest in these necessary reforms, but although many junior high schools changed their names to middle schools, they didn't change their internal operations in any significant way. As with other reform efforts, there were no written guidelines to help teachers and administrators translate the ideas and philosophy into action on a day-to-day basis. Teachers and students had no guides to help them make fundamental changes to what they knew as teaching and learning.

Several things happened in the 1980s to move the middle school reform movement forward. One was the publication of Joan Lipsitz's book *Successful Schools for Young Adolescents* (1984), which noted that exemplary middle schools were characterized by a recognition of young adolescent needs, an interdisciplinary approach to learning, and the replacement of traditional teaching methods with learner-centered approaches. One state after another, as well as national educational organizations (see Middle Grade Task Force [1987], National Association of Secondary School Principals [1985], National Middle School Association [1989], and Vermont Middle Grades Task Force [1991]), began to produce similar, if not identical, recommendations for middle schools. The Carnegie Council on Adolescent Development report titled *Turning Points: Preparing American Youth for the 21st Century* (1989) described traditional education as a mismatch between instructional methods and the needs of young adolescents. One of the main recommendations reads as follows:

> *Teach young adolescents to think critically.* Contrary to conventional belief, young adolescents can learn to think critically. Developing reasoning abilities requires greater reliance by teachers on learning techniques that allow students to participate actively in discovering and creating their own solutions to problems. Teaching subjects grouped around integrating themes, for example, can help students to see systems rather than disconnected facts. Testing of students' learning should require students to demonstrate the full range of thinking skills, rather than mere retention of facts. (Carnegie Council on Adolescent Development, 1989, p. 13)

Finally, James Beane (1993), a nationally recognized leader in the middle school movement, concludes that although reform efforts have addressed middle school organizational issues, very few changes have occurred in middle school curriculum or teaching approaches. Without these fundamental changes, Beane believes, even dramatic structural and organizational changes will not significantly alter the learning experience of young adolescents. Although he refers to meddling with the issues of curriculum and teaching approaches as "risky business" (p. 2), nothing in his view is more fundamental than that curriculum should address the needs of early adolescents. In his view, this means that middle schools must provide opportunities for students to play a major role in developing a curriculum based on questions and concerns they have about themselves and their world.

Dick and Jane Are Growing Up, Are Bored to Death, and Need to Plan for Their Future

Reform at the High School Level

If you teach at the high school level, you probably deal daily with the apathy and lethargy of teenagers. If you are not a high school teacher, you might want to visit a typical high school. In many traditional schools, you will find students slouching in their seats, or off task, or with their heads down on their desks, or causing mayhem, or simply zoning out. We need to do better. High school students are our immediate futures.

In contrast, if you visit schools where constructivist philosophies and formats have changed or are changing the instructional process, you will be more apt to see very engaged teenagers who become annoyed when they have to stop working. There is no one more responsible for positive changes at the high school level than Ted Sizer (1984, 1996) of the Coalition of Essential Schools. From describing the dilemmas of Horace, the composite high school teacher, to developing an organization that defines guidelines and propositions for schools that want to make changes, Sizer's ideas have become the foundation for reform in high schools. At the core of his thinking are two central ideas: Students need to be in charge of their own learning, and content learning needs to be as integrated as possible.

More recently, the Carnegie Foundation joined forces with the National Association of Secondary School Principals (NASSP) to study teaching/learning and restructuring issues at the high school level. The NASSP published *Breaking Ranks: Changing an American Institution* (1996), the overriding theme of which is that schools need to be learner focused rather than textbook or teacher focused. The report recommends changes in organizational structure (for example, moving to block scheduling) similar to the changes advised for middle schools by the Carnegie Report *Turning Points* (1989). The NASSP report recommends that

- Learning experiences engage students actively in thinking, discovering, problem solving, and developing their own knowledge
- Academic standards be rigorous
- Subjects be integrated whenever possible
- Teachers be facilitators of learning rather than simply information deliverers

All these proposals are core to constructivist approaches.

Professional Teachers' Organizations

To understand just how mainstream constructivism has become (at least in theory, if not in practice), one needs only to look at how professional teachers' organizations have embraced constructivist ideas. In fact, the common thread in all the new discipline-area standard frameworks is emphasis on learning rather than on the teaching process. The new national standards are the results of intensive projects involving different groups of people including educators, researchers, parents, and policy makers. All have tried to frame the major concepts and themes of the field rather than to make exhaustive lists (ad nauseam) of everyone's desired content, which cannot possibly be written in any meaningful way.

NCTE: English/Language Arts

In 1993, the National Council of Teachers of English (NCTE) reported that the methods for teaching literature in secondary schools still remained quite traditional. They described this approach as teacher dominated and revolving around whole-class discussions that were meant to direct students to one common understanding. The new *Standards for the English Language Arts*, which were developed by the National Council of Teachers of English and International Reading Association (1996), propose to change this traditional approach to a learner-centered focus. The standards advocate problem solving and application in real situations.

NCTM: Math

As with the other new national standards, those from the National Council of Teachers of Mathematics (NCTM) argue that current traditional practices have to change and that we can no longer accept that our students need problem solving "only on Wednesdays," as was reported by one of our graduate students in a survey he did of local teacher practice. The focus of *Curriculum and Evaluation Standards for School Mathematics* (NCTM, 1992) is on active learning; these standards stress that students need to discover why formulas and procedures work rather than how to follow them, to understand rather than memorize, to create and solve math problems related to real life, and to move from thinking that there is one right answer to focusing on mathematical reasoning. The companion booklet, *Assessment Standards for School Mathematics* (NCTM, 1995), reiterates that there needs to be a shift in emphasis from students listening and memorizing to student inquiry and investigation. This document blames traditional methods for perpetuating the myth that some students simply can't do math. It defines the teacher's role as questioning, listening, and setting high expectations, and it describes assessment as a way to determine students' understanding and as a stepping-stone to future learning.

NSTA: Science

The same themes in the latest science standards have been framed in a single phrase: *Science as inquiry*. As with studies reported by the NCTE, findings from a 1993 survey of science and math education showed that although hands-on activities have increased in science classes, the largest proportion of class time in science is still spent listening to lecture (Association for Supervision and Curriculum Development [ASCD], 1995). The new standards developed by the National Science Teachers Association (NSTA) encourage students to make meaning for themselves through active investigation (ASCD, 1995); the *National Science Education Standards* also focus on learning science as an active process (ASCD, 1995) and on student understanding and use of investigative and problem-solving processes (National Academy of Sciences, 1996).

NCSS: Social Studies

The National History Standards (National Center for History in the Schools, 1994) and the revised standards (1996) focus on students finding and interpreting records and constructing solid historical arguments and conclusions. *Charting a Course: Social Studies for the 21st Century*, the report of the National Commission on Social Studies in the Schools (1989) not only proposes active learning (researching, organizing, and analyzing and interpreting data) but also goes so far as to suggest that students should develop their own curricular materials (Page, 1992).

Ho-Hum and So What?

Yes, most of us have heard much of this before. The problem now is the same as it has been in the past. There are few guidelines to help teachers make the transition from the traditional approach to teaching and learning to an active approach. Before we move to models you can try, you need to do some diagnostic work on Your Own Classroom in Chapter 4.

Tough Questions

1. If one out of five students requires more explicit phonics instruction (but four out of five may be bored to tears with this approach), how can we set up our classrooms to meet the needs of all children?

2. At what age should we assume (if there is *any* age) that a child's failure to discover spelling and phonics patterns means we should switch gears and provide direct instruction? That is, if a child is not discovering phonemic patterns naturally, how long should we wait before we try a more teacher-directed approach?

3. At what age/grade should teachers become less forgiving with invented spelling and expect more precision in student writing? Why?

4. Susan Jackson understood the constructivist ideas advocated in the middle school reform efforts. Her knowledge base included much about appropriate middle school organization, the needs of young adolescents, interdisciplinary teaming, constructivist learning theory, and student developed curriculum. Based on her letter (Chapter 1) written at the beginning of her teaching experience in a middle school, in what way(s) had her teacher preparation program failed her?

5. It appears that reform efforts are the slowest at the high school level. Why do you think this might be so?

6. If all the professional teachers' organizations have developed standards grounded in constructivist propositions, why haven't classrooms made drastic changes to meet these standards? How would you go about creating a plan in your school to address the standards?

7. Is integrating subject matter more difficult at the high school level? Why? How can this practice be encouraged without causing "turf" battles and feelings of inadequacy in teachers who believe they are not qualified to introduce concepts from other academic disciplines?

Four

Look Before You Leap

With some of the theory and the history of school reform movements associated with constructivism behind us, it's time to start thinking about where you are on your journey toward setting up a constructivist classroom. Becoming a constructivist teacher often requires a change in attitude about how students learn and an appreciation for the conditions that motivate learning (as opposed to those that simply motivate performance). It also may require a change in the way you think about your role in helping students learn. This chapter is designed to help you shift mental gears. To make the demands of this cognitive shift more concrete, we begin the chapter with checklists that relate to constructivist classrooms; these should provide both an opportunity for reflection and a point of departure for your journey.

In this chapter, we discuss some of the core components of constructivist classrooms. Some of these relate directly to the checklists. We will examine how what you say, even to yourself, affects the way your students and you approach teaching and learning. We will offer a constructivist framework for thinking about teacher and student roles, the assessment of student learning, and the important connections between student choice and classroom management. Although we have broken down these questions into various categories, you should notice pretty early on that these topics are all interrelated.

Looking at Your Own Classroom:
Where Are You Now?

Review Checklists 4.1 to 4.6 and indicate how often each statement is true.

CHECKLIST 4.1

Classroom Language	Always	Almost Always	Some-times	Hardly Ever
I use the words "discover" or "uncover" instead of "cover."	____	____	____	____
I use the words "investigation" or "exploration" instead of "unit."	____	____	____	____
I use the word "learn" instead of "teach."	____	____	____	____
I use the phrase "learning experience" instead of "presentation."	____	____	____	____
I use the phrase "student learning plan" instead of "lesson plan."	____	____	____	____

CHECKLIST 4.2

The Communication System	Always	Almost Always	Some-times	Hardly Ever
My classroom communication system is reciprocal rather than teacher directed.	——	——	——	——
Students spend more time engaged in their own work than listening to me talk.	——	——	——	——
Teacher talk is in the form of questions rather than directives.	——	——	——	——
If a stranger walked into the room, he/she would be more likely to hear students' voices than mine.	——	——	——	——
I do less talking than the students.	——	——	——	——
Questions posed by me or the students don't have a single-word answer.	——	——	——	——
Students can use their normal voices to get my or their classmates' attention (i.e., they do not have to raise their voices).	——	——	——	——
Students feel comfortable turning to each other for help.	——	——	——	——
I can use my normal voice to get students' attention.	——	——	——	——

CHECKLIST 4.3

Roles, Activity, and Management	Always	Almost Always	Some-times	Hardly Ever
I encourage students to find answers to their own questions.	___	___	___	___
I see myself as a facilitator rather than as an information dispenser.	___	___	___	___
I see students as decision makers.	___	___	___	___
Students have a say in the daily schedule.	___	___	___	___
The classroom is free of daydreaming, inattention, boredom, alienation, and rebellion.	___	___	___	___
If I have a concern about a student's behavior, I view it as an opportunity for discussion, resolution, and problem solving.	___	___	___	___
Students work together to discuss classroom management issues.	___	___	___	___
When things fall apart, I take this as an opportunity for the class to discuss solutions to what I and others may see as problematic.	___	___	___	___

CHECKLIST 4.4

Classroom Physical Environment	Always	Almost Always	Some-times	Hardly Ever
Students fill the walls with their work.	———	———	———	———
We arrange the furniture to be conducive to student learning.	———	———	———	———
The physical layout of the room allows me to get every-one's attention if needed.	———	———	———	———
We move the furniture accord-ing to what we are doing.	———	———	———	———
Students and I feel safe in this classroom.	———	———	———	———
Students have a say in what the classroom looks like.	———	———	———	———

CHECKLIST 4.5

Motivation	Always	Almost Always	Some-times	Hardly Ever
I avoid the use of threats of punishment.	——	——	——	——
I avoid promising rewards.	——	——	——	——
Students pursue topics independently, take initiative, or engage in additional activities related to—but above and beyond—what we are studying.	——	——	——	——
The students realize that they are responsible for their own thinking and learning.	——	——	——	——
Students are disappointed when an activity, lesson, or period ends.	——	——	——	——
Students stay late to discuss their work.	——	——	——	——
Students leave my classroom engaged in conversation about the last thing they were working on.	——	——	——	——
Students are rarely absent.	——	——	——	——
Students look forward to class.	——	——	——	——
My students and I think of the classroom as our class, rather than as my class.	——	——	——	——

CHECKLIST 4.6

Assessment	Always	Almost Always	Some-times	Hardly Ever
If a student went down the hall to explain what we were working on, why it was important, and what it is like that she's done before, this would not be a problem.	⎯⎯	⎯⎯	⎯⎯	⎯⎯
Students have a hand in creating assessment tools and criteria.	⎯⎯	⎯⎯	⎯⎯	⎯⎯
Students know at the beginning of new units what form the assessment will take.	⎯⎯	⎯⎯	⎯⎯	⎯⎯
Students believe assessment is an opportunity to learn more, not a way to measure one student against another.	⎯⎯	⎯⎯	⎯⎯	⎯⎯
Students understand how the assessments we use connect to what we do in class.	⎯⎯	⎯⎯	⎯⎯	⎯⎯

Count 4 for each *Always*, 3 for each *Almost Always*, 2 for each *Sometimes*, and 1 for each *Hardly Ever*. If you scored between 43 (the minimum score) and 80, there is bad news and good news. The bad news is that you have a lot of work to do before your class is constructivist; the good news is you have nowhere to go but up. If you scored between 80 and 120, you are already making progress toward creating a constructivist class; keep going. If you scored between 120 and 160, you are definitely making strides and probably can use this book to support and confirm what you are already doing. If you scored above 160, give this book to someone else who needs it.

Explaining Basic Components

What Language Do You Use in Your Classroom?

If you have tried already to make the shift from a traditional classroom to an active learning environment and have had less than expected results, or if you want to try to make some changes now, first you will need to look at subtle and not so subtle dynamics in your classroom. We will start by asking you to review five words or phrases that are key to making changes in your classroom. We will do this in the form of a challenge to you. Table 4.1 is only half complete. The side that is filled in represents the language you and students perhaps use and hear in a traditional classroom. We would recommend some kind of penance if we thought it would help you to eliminate it. What it *will* take is tremendous concentration and discipline on your part to make some changes here. Fill in the constructivist half of the table with language you think will lead to a different focus and a more student-engaged and powered dynamic. See Table 4.2 to see the changes we would recommend.

Why These Changes?

The language that most teachers use is the language they know; that is the language they experienced themselves as students. That language has its origin in the traditional, behaviorist system, which more often than not defines learning as acquiring, accumulating, and memorizing. Traditional language not only does not work in a constructivist classroom but also hinders creation and sustenance of constructivism. The changes we recommend here will force you to keep the emphasis where it belongs: on the learner and learning, rather than on the teacher and teaching.

Clarifying the Changes

Review the following:

1. Change "teaching" to "learning." Force yourself to rephrase every sentence, question, and thought in which you use a form of the words "teach," "teaching," or "teacher" to use a form of the words "learn," "learning," or "learner." Instead of asking yourself how you can *teach* Johnnie to do long division, change the question to: "What

TABLE 4.1 Traditional Language

Traditional	*Constructivist*
1a. Today I will be *teaching* about the Civil War.	
1b. Tomorrow I need to *teach* about subtraction.	
2a. I never write *lesson plans*.	
2b. I always have to change my *lesson plans*.	
3a. I have to *cover* fractions this week.	
3b. We have the departmental exam in February, so I have to *cover* half the textbook by then.	
4a. What *unit* are you working on?	
4b. We can start the Shakespeare *unit* on Monday.	
5a. Next week your *presentations* will begin.	
5b. How many of you have your *presentations* ready?	

TABLE 4.2 Constructivist Language

Traditional	Constructivist
1. Today I will be *teaching* about the Civil War.	Today you (the students) will be *learning* about the Civil War.
2. I have to change my *lesson plans*.	You have to modify your *learning plans*.
3. I have to *cover* fractions this week.	Next week, you will *discover* how fractions work.
4. What *unit* are you working on?	What are you *investigating*?
5. How many of you have your *presentations* ready?	How many of you have your *interactive learning experiences (ILEs)* ready?

is the best way for Johnnie to *learn* division?" This forces a shift in your thinking and puts the focus on Johnnie and his abilities/talents/challenges. This simple, yet not so simple, word substitution will generate further questioning and thinking by you and may lead to a constructivist approach to learning. Remember, you can *teach* students anything, but it doesn't mean they have *learned* a thing.

2. Change your "lesson plan" to a "student learning plan." Here again, the idea is to shift the focus from you to the students, from teaching to learning. To change your written plans, especially if you are a new teacher, you may need to create two plans. One will become your agenda—the list of things you will do during the class or day. The other becomes the students' learning plan. It could look something like the plan in Box 4.1.

3. Change "cover" to "discover" or "uncover." Of all the traditional classroom language we hear teachers use, this is the deadliest. As long as you "cover" curriculum, you won't be able to establish a constructivist learning environment. It's not that content is not important; it is extremely important, but in a constructivist classroom, a teacher does not stand and deliver all or even much of the content.

Box 4.1: Student Learning Plan

Topic:	*Causes of the Civil War*
Student Learning Objective:	Students *will demonstrate understanding* of the causes of the Civil War.
Learning Activity:	Students will work in pairs. Each student in a pair will conduct specific and different research related to the causes of the Civil War. Susie will review newspaper reports of the time period and draw conclusions about the causes of the Civil War; her partner, Sandy, will conduct research on the Internet to determine different viewpoints on the causes of the war. Similarly, other pairs will define their research. The more different the research assignments are in the different pairs, the more thorough the learning for the whole class.
Student Demonstration of Understanding	To demonstrate understanding of the causes of the Civil War, students will draw cartoons that analyze the causes OR Students will create a video (or skit) that analyzes different perspectives of the causes OR Students will be involved in . . . any activity that allows you to discern student understanding, not simply recall of information.

Instead, students uncover, discover, and reflect on content through inquiry, research, and analysis in the context of a problem, critical question, issue, procedure, or theme. Heed the advice and warning of an experienced teacher:

> Covering content or curriculum is like putting a lid on a pot. We shouldn't be putting a lid on the pot; students should be taking the lid off the pot and figuring out what's in it, what it means, and why. (White in Page, 1992, p. 212)

4. Change "unit" to "investigation" or "exploration." Can you think of a more boring or inactive word than "unit"? Who could possibly get excited by that word or concept? If you are trying to incor-

porate active learning into your classroom, you need to get rid of that word and find an action word to take its place. It needs to be a word that conveys in some way the central learning activity. We have suggested "investigation" or "exploration." You can think of others. The trick is to pay attention to when you are using the word "unit" and force yourself to make the change. If you put the two words "unit" and "investigation" side by side, what happens in your mind? What would you guess happens in students' minds? Which phrase naturally leads to action? Which phrase makes you think of questioning and problem solving? Which phrase makes you want to do something?

5. Change "presentations" to "interactive learning experiences." (Boy, what a mouthful. Can you think of a better phrase to mean the same thing? We'd love to hear from you.) Let's assume you want your students to become active learners who develop their own knowledge. Let's also assume that your students decided to conduct an investigation, carried it out successfully, synthesized and analyzed the new material, drew conclusions, and raised new questions. Those activities would constitute an active learning/constructivist exercise. If you then ask the students to make a presentation on their learning experience, you will put the class into the position of being receivers of information—just as they would be if you were giving the information. The investigators have had a constructivist experience, but the presentation becomes exactly the type of experience (for the rest of the class) that you are trying to avoid!

How boring can student presentations be? Very, very boring! Students can learn, nevertheless, just as most educators are having to learn, that there are ways for students to lead learning experiences that actively involve the rest of the class. As long as you call an activity a presentation, though, that's what you will get: a presentation—someone presenting and everyone else receiving. Instead, you can explain to students that they are now the experts in the topic, and their job is to think of an activity that they can conduct with the rest of the class that will allow the class members to be actively involved in learning about the topic.

Although the age of your students will make some difference here, we have seen pre-service and experienced teachers do this successfully with children who are only in the 2nd grade. One way to develop this sort of task is to ask for the students' ideas on how this could happen. Another is to reflect on components of active learning experiences you develop for the class and figure out how students can learn to use those same components as they develop interactive learning experiences for the class.

Using new language won't cure all the problems of making the shift from a traditional classroom to a constructivist one, but if you don't change your language, you will have a difficult time shifting your thinking. No teacher can speak in a traditional language and expect to have a constructivist classroom.

Your Classroom Communication System

Top to Bottom or Side By Side?

Think about the verbal exchanges common in your own class-room, or think back to those that took place when you were a student. Here's an exchange familiar to many traditional classrooms. When a student asks a teacher about a subject about which the teacher has little background information, a traditional teacher might say, "You don't need to know that." What might the teacher be communicating here?

1. The information you request will not be part of any future exam constructed by me or the Educational Testing Service.
2. I don't know; therefore, you don't need to know.
3. I don't know, and I am embarrassed to tell you that I don't know (because after all I *am* the teacher and I *am* supposed to know everything).
4. I know everything, including whether or not the information you request is relevant to your life.

Fill in the blank: What do *you* mean if/when you tell students, "You don't need to know"?

In a constructivist classroom, on the other hand, the student/teacher communication system is a reciprocal one. For example, in the scenario described above, the teacher might respond, "I don't know, how could we find out?" Students and teachers both initiate classroom dialogue and raise questions. Constructivist communication systems respect the students' ability to start or add to a discussion and to ask productive questions. In contrast, in traditional classrooms, as Freire (1974) would say, the student/teacher communication system is a vertical one in which the teacher at the top is responsible for transmitting messages to the students at the bottom. This system sends the message that students cannot figure things out for themselves and that the teacher knows everything.

Noise

Another aspect of the student/teacher communication system is noise. If noise is anything that interferes with a message, then there is more noise (interference) in a traditional classroom communication system than in a constructivist one. The noise in a traditional classroom includes daydreaming, inattention, visual distractions, misunderstandings, boredom, lack of motivation, alienation, and rebellion. In a constructivist communication classroom system, in which the teacher and students are both senders and receivers, both teachers and learners, there is constant clarification, interpretation, and re-creation of messages. This communication system, which leads to student engagement, eliminates most of the noise of a traditional classroom even though student voices may fill the classroom.

Student/Teacher Roles

Don't Give Up Your Responsibility

A constructivist student/teacher communication system does not mean, however, that the teacher gives up responsibility. Although a major role for students in a constructivist classroom is to direct their own learning, they do not have license to do whatever they want. The teacher's role is to guide, focus, suggest, lead, and continually evaluate the progress of the students. Yes, the role of the teacher also is to provide direct instruction. The question is how much direction, how much intervention, and how much direct instruction is necessary. You as the teacher have the experience and the expertise. You also have the responsibility to determine whether or not the learning process is heading to a relevant and academically productive conclusion, and you need to take the necessary steps to ensure that this occurs.

Teacher/Student Collaboration

In a traditional classroom, you might see a teacher who stands in front of the room, does most of the talking, and tries to fill the heads of her students, like so many empty vessels. This is not what we see when we visit—and we visit whenever we can—Jan Carpenter's 1-2 multi-age classroom in Vermont. It takes a few minutes to find Jan. There is no clear front or back of the room, and there is always a quiet buzz of activity. Students are working together around small round tables, or problem solving in a corner of the room, or reading to each other, or sharing ideas about how to solve a puzzle. Many different activities appear to be taking place simultaneously, and Jan . . . well, she's hard to find, but she's in the room. Like her students, Jan is also actively engaged in whatever the class is working on—observing a reaction at a science center, talking with students about their plans for a new learning center, or working on the computer with students trying to solve a math puzzle. Jan sees herself as a learner, and her enthusiasm for learning serves as both a model for and a mirror of the high levels of active engagement taking place in her classroom.

In constructivist classrooms like Jan's, teachers see themselves, describe themselves, and act as collaborators, team leaders, and guides—not as information dispensers, bosses, or disciplinarians. Constructivist teachers ask rather than tell, they model rather than explain, and they work as hard as possible to get out of the limelight so that their students may shine. This means that you will not always direct classroom dialogue, but instead students will do the initiating. It means that you will no longer be the single, or even the most important, audience when students speak. You will not be the only judge of student work; students will learn to evaluate other students' work as well as their own.

The test of your effectiveness will not concern your oratorical skill, your ability to tell a good story, or your ability to prepare a clear and compelling lecture (although you need these skills); nor will it concern your ability to entertain students with scientific discovery, or mathematical prowess, or gripping and bloody tales of historical battles. A good constructivist teacher—in our view, a *good teacher*—is one who provides opportunities for students to become the great orators, storytellers, historians, mathematicians, and scientists. Students do not become great scientists by listening to the teacher tell them about what great science is, they become great scientists by having the opportunity to do science.

Students Who Resist

What about students who like their old roles, or who are more comfortable listening than telling, or who are interested in learning only if it is "on the test," or who are afraid to try something on their own for fear it is not what the teacher wants? If left in traditional settings long enough, students often will balk at opportunities for real decision making—after all, it takes more work than simply listening to a teacher tell you what to do, and it can involve more risk. Students may say, "You're the teacher, you tell us!" More outrageously, they may say, "Well, if we have a say, then let's all just do whatever we want, whenever we want." Some teachers view such statements as a call for help, or as an unconscious plea for structure and discipline, or as an example that students cannot be responsible for making good decisions. We see such statements, however, as precious opportunities for class discussion, for group problem solving, and for students to learn how to be independent thinkers and doers.

Decision Making in Jan Carpenter's Room

Jan recently introduced a new series of math problems, and she asked the class how they should proceed. One student suggested they break into small groups, another that they choose partners, and a third, Marcy, suggested that Ms. Carpenter present the problems to the class as a whole and that whenever anyone had an idea about how to solve a particular problem, he or she could just call it out. Several students thought Marcy's plan was best and said so.

Jan asked, "How would Marcy's plan work? What do you think would happen if everyone called out an answer at once?" None of the students responded. Jan said, "Let's try Marcy's idea. After all, how will we know if this is a good plan until we try it?" After presenting the first problem, six students called out simultaneously. Jan asked, "What did you say?" In response, the six students repeated their responses but were now joined by several others who sought to help out Jan and their classmates. Each tried to speak more loudly than his or her peers. A loud racket ensued. After several moments, Jan asked, "Is this a good plan?" Many students answered: "No." Jan asked, "Why not?" A productive discussion followed, and the class, as a group, arrived at a more useful way of handling the day's work.

Classroom Management

Managing a classroom is crucial for developing and sustaining any classroom system, including a constructivist classroom. If you don't create a safe environment for everyone, your classroom won't be productive, regardless of the teaching/learning approach you follow. Two components are critical to successfully managing any class-room: engaging students in meaningful and relevant active academic tasks and responding to distracting student behavior in the classroom.

The more engaged students are in relevant activity, the less will be the disruptive student behavior; the less students are actively en-gaged, the more disruptive student behavior there will be. This raises some interesting questions for the constructivist classroom. Simply encouraging students to make their own choices does not mean they will automatically become engaged and stay on task. In fact, because they are so used to being in a different kind of class-room system, they may translate your ideas about choice and stu-dent directed learning in the following ways:

"Boy, is this teacher weak."

"This teacher doesn't have a clue."

"This will be a ball—we can do whatever we want."

If you try to make a revolutionary change in your classroom, most likely you will end up with a classroom in chaos. Do you think this might be what happened to Susan (Chapter 1)? Did she try to do too much that was too different too fast? The change has to be gradual. It has to evolve slowly, with constant explanation of why you are making the changes and what you expect. When students feel that the classroom is their room, that decisions about the sequence and scope of their activities are made with their input, classroom man-agement becomes increasingly what its name implies: a method for organizing the complex array of activities that occur in school classrooms, as opposed to strenuous attempts to discipline, control, or punish students.

Classroom management, like reading and writing, is a skill that takes time to develop. In a constructivist classroom, students themselves gradually acquire good management skills when they have the op-portunity to practice them.

Classroom Physical Environment

Although a certain seating arrangement may be more or less con-ducive to constructivist approaches, seating arrangements in and of themselves tell you little. Students sitting in rows can be mentally active working on a problem. That would be constructivist. Students can be sitting at tables or sitting in a circle or on the floor without this meaning anything in terms of what the students are or are not learning. You have to know what they are doing and whether or not they are on task and thinking. If students are sitting in a circle and following a teacher-prescribed lesson and format, then it is probably not constructivist. If the students are sitting in groups at tables but are thinking about what is going to happen on Saturday night . . . well, you get the idea.

Student Choice

Likewise, how much choosing the students get to do does not necessarily tell you whether you have a constructivist activity. One way to look at the issue of choice is to say: There are some times a student has no choice. This can relate to curriculum requirements, standardized testing, safety issues in the classroom, or a certain book to read. There are times when a student can have total choice. This could be choice of topic related to a bigger theme, choice of research method, choice of demonstration of understanding, or choice of creating a new formula, a new process, or new experiments. There are times when you and the students will decide on things together. This could be the overriding theme, the culminating activity, or the form of assessment. Again, what is important can be framed as a question: What are the students doing? Are they figuring something out, trying to create, invent, analyze, or synthesize? Keep in mind that constructivist activities often can be embedded in what appears to be a very traditional framework. Again, this is a solid way to begin your class changes.

Assessing Student Learning

Assessment and Instruction

Students may work in large groups, in small teams, in pairs, independently . . . but you will no longer be the sole yardstick by which they will measure their progress. In constructivist classrooms, teachers help students to monitor themselves, to monitor their own progress, to establish criteria for learning and for quality work, and to devise their own remedial plans. Assessment is not separate from instruction; assessment is a continuous process that drives instruction and is embedded within it (Kugelmass, 1995). Assessment does not bring an end to learning; it provides information about how to continue with respect to learning and curriculum requirements.

Are Quizzes Constructivist?

Traditional assessment formats, such as multiple choice exams, often require students, either through processes of recognition or recall, to indicate what they have memorized. As such, traditional testing formats may be good measures of what students remember; rarely, however, are they good measures of what students can do or of what they understand. But they could be. The question to keep in mind is this: What are students doing? Having a test or a quiz in a classroom does not tell you whether the class is constructivist or not. You would have to look at the quiz or test to determine that. Does the quiz/test require student understanding? Does it require that students apply their knowledge? For example: "List the most important rules of capitalization" is a typical traditional test question and does not require understanding. On the other hand, "Create two sentences using two different rules of capitalization and then explain what the rules and uses are in your sentences" requires student understanding. Test/quizzes can be a combination of both traditional and constructivist formats. Using this combination might be a good way to make the transition for students.

Demonstration of Understanding

Ultimately, you should be thinking about assessment as an active demonstration of student understanding and ability to apply this understanding. Think about the assessment process one must undergo to obtain a driver's license. Although a multiple choice exam may be a useful way to assess whether a potential driver remembers the right sequence of steps to parallel park a car, few people would feel comfortable saying that strong performance on such a test indicates good parallel parking ability. To create assessment instruments that do more than merely tap a student's recall or recognition skills, we must reframe assessment so that

- It is, as much as possible, a continuous process that is part of instruction and not separate from it.
- It connects directly to learning and is introduced before or simultaneously with material.

- It requires students to do more than simply remember (e.g., requires students to develop mathematical formulas, produce exhibitions, write essays, create a sculpture, write poetry, create a musical score, develop and participate in debates, or create and conduct experiments).
- Student questions, at least in part, drive the process.

Having described what assessments ideally should look like, we must also keep in mind that there is a danger in becoming too concerned with assessment per se. The single most important question we should really be asking about testing student learning is not *how* we should be doing assessments but *why* we are doing them. If the answer has less to do with student learning and more to do with making comparative judgments, we're on the wrong track. As Kohn has pointed out in *Punished by Rewards* (1993), a vast body of research indicates that as students become increasingly concerned with *how* they are doing, they become decreasingly concerned with *what* they are doing. The focus should be on learning, on how it is done, and on how it can be better, not on normative comparisons. Kohn (1996) suggests:

> Ask the students how they can best show you, when we finish . . . , what they've understood, what they need help with, what questions they had answered, and what new questions they have. . . . If you are doing grades or tests, make as little a deal about it as possible. The last thing you want to do is talk about good grades as a cause for celebration or stickers. Rather, we'll talk about how it could have been better, how my teaching could have improved, how your learning can improve next week, and then we move on. Otherwise, the grade or the grade substitute becomes the point. (p. 5)

This chapter provides much to think about in terms of getting ready to make some changes in your classroom. In the next chapter, we will discuss the issues of content and standards; describe how to prepare your students, their parents, and the principal for changes you are going to make; and then describe step-by-step models you can implement. Before jumping ahead, try out the following Tough Questions.

Tough Questions

1. Neither the constructivist (reciprocal) classroom communication system nor the student/teacher roles in a constructivist classroom translate into a concrete job description for the teacher. Because every activity, every class, and every student is different, how can teachers develop a checklist that will allow them to ensure that the active learning environment will exist or will work?

2. In the constructivist classroom, how will you know how much learning the student is doing?

3. If discovery is continually reshaped and reinterpreted through teacher intervention, how much learning is really the student's?

4. How does a teacher determine if what the student is learning involves erroneous concepts or inappropriate data?

5. How can you avoid a situation in which much of a student's search for solutions, new procedures, or conclusions is really the search for what the student thinks is the teacher's right solution or what the teacher is looking for?

6. How important are normative, standardized assessments in which a student's performance is compared to other students her age? Are these without any value? Are they really less important than judgments made by you and your students? Isn't it valuable to know whether a student's performance is much better or worse than that of her age cohorts around the country, region, state, county, or school?

7. How important are standards? How would you respond to community pressure to increase scores on nationally standardized tests?

8. Active learning is time-consuming. How do you accommodate for this?

9. How would you respond to a teacher who says: "I will not hand over my teacher-centered classroom. Why should I? I've been teaching Greek mythology, or Algebra II, or American History or . . . (fill in the blank) for 20 years. Of course I know more about these subjects than they do."

10. What does this mean: [SM—RM]? (Sless, 1981). *Hint:* It's about communication.

Five

Back to the *Real Basics*

The Content/Process Hullabaloo

Before you try to implement one or more of the models in Chapter 6, it is important that we discuss the issue of content in the constructivist classroom. This is one of the most misunderstood of the constructivist concepts. Traditional teachers as well as parents often think there is no connected content in a constructivist class. This misunderstanding might result from lack of information, or, worse, it might be because content in what a teacher calls a constructivist class has gone awry.

Content in a Constructivist Classroom: Where's the Beef?

Educational reformers often say, "The process *is* the content." Although they do this to emphasize the importance of problem solving and critical thinking processes, it can lead others to believe that content is not important or that reformers *think* that content is not important. This is not the case in a constructivist class; content is very important. The difference between a traditional class and a constructivist class in relation to content is not whether content is important or whether there is content; it is in the way in which students interact with, come to learn, and come to understand content. Before you begin to implement any of the models, you need to be clear that you will not be abandoning content; you also need to make it clear to students that they will be learning about content topics in a different way.

Mind Shift

Here is where your mind shift becomes key to any changes in your classroom. Let's see where you are, using Checklist 5.1.

CHECKLIST 5.1

Beliefs About Students	*Agree*	*Disagree*
Students are capable of questioning, investigating, thinking, and discovering for themselves.	_____	_____
All students can think critically at some level.	_____	_____
Teachers should help students to become independent thinkers/doers.	_____	_____
Students need to believe in their own ability.	_____	_____
Students cannot develop their own meaning or knowledge or perspectives about issues, or learn to make decisions, simply by absorbing the teacher's information.	_____	_____
A democratic society requires citizens that can think independently.	_____	_____
Students have the ability to take responsibility for their own learning.	_____	_____
Students are capable of conducting interviews, publishing their work, writing scripts, and producing TV presentations.	_____	_____

You have to believe that students are capable of doing great things. If all of your check marks are in the "agree" column, you definitely are ready to try some models and probably already have some active learning models of your own. If you have some check marks in the "disagree" column, try the simplest model for as long as it takes you to see that students are truly capable of doing surprising things. When you discover this, review this checklist again, then try a model in which you give up more control or in which students do more complex things. The important issue here is that for students to work with content in a new way, you have to believe they can.

Agreeing on Curriculum Content

Even if teaching were about *covering* content, which it is not, there is no universal agreement on what that content should be. If you get 20 teachers together and ask them what topics students absolutely cannot live without or cannot be considered educated without (at any grade level for any subject), good luck finding agreement. Add parents, school board members, and administrators to this group of teachers and you can expect many deadlocks and disagreements, even shouting matches. If this group does come up with a list, it undoubtedly will be a very long one. If you then ask why each of these topics is absolutely essential or how each topic relates to the students' future lives, careers, or to our future citizenry maintaining and creating a better society . . . well, good luck again. Opinions on this matter are like textbooks; unfortunately, everyone seems to have one.

Developing Curriculum

It's that word *cover* that skews any discussion of curriculum content. Even when teachers are in a school system that asks them to develop the curriculum, the questions they raise usually are about what can and should be covered and when. This is the language with which they are familiar. The longer the list of required or recommended topics, the more apt teachers are to feel pressure to teach by telling—to avoid learning experiences that are time-consuming and student driven. Surely teachers' goals do not include burying students in an avalanche of information, but this often is what happens.

What's Changing?

There is good news. Many of the new national, state, and professional organization standards frameworks—as explained in Chapter 3—have tried to present major themes, ideas, and concepts rather than long lists of topics. This is because these frameworks are constructivist-based and stress the importance of, and advocate that students are involved in, active learning. These frameworks are meant to be flexible so that teachers and schools can make their own decisions about specific content topics in relation to the overarching themes and can use active learning methods more readily. If you are using a curriculum framework—whether developed by the school, the state, an organization, or teachers—that looks like the table of contents from a traditional textbook, then probably that will become your syllabus, and you will feel pressure to *cover* the material.

Letting Go

Letting go of your favorite topic to allow for more in-depth attention and a different kind of learning for students in fewer areas can be painful and scary. It will be the most difficult action shift you have to make. It is necessary because students need the opportunity to uncover the curriculum, not cover it. Which do you think is more important and more valuable:

a. Dispensing thousands of bits of information that the student won't remember anyway.

OR

b. Having students work on one or a few topics or problems in depth and develop their own, and sustainable, knowledge and understanding?

Keep in mind as you think about this that in 90 days students forget 90% of everything they have been told (Smilovitz, 1996).

Back to the *Real Basics*

As we said in Chapter 2, the *real basics* are old. The *real basics* are not about what you teach (tell) but about how and what students learn. Direct instruction and student memorization always will be necessary to some degree; the questions are to what degree and in what areas? To answer these questions, we need to start with what we know. We know that active learning—that is, when students do their own investigating, figuring out, and creating—is the most effective kind of learning. We also know that active learning approaches are time-consuming. That is why you cannot have a long list of content and have much active learning going on. You have heard the "less is more" proposition: That is, with fewer topics, there is greater possibility for rich connections and in-depth learning. Because students do make richer connections and integrate a variety of subjects, the "less is more approach" actually leads to students learning more content, which in turn means that you need to do less direct instruction.

Reviewing Your Own Curriculum Content

There are two things you need to do to get back to the *real basics*, that is, to create a constructivist classroom. First, you have to review your curriculum content requirements. Second, you have to learn how to weave content together. If your curriculum is a list of topics, ask yourself (about each topic) the same thing that students ask: Why do we need to know, study, or do this? If you can't come up with any response besides "because it's required," it's time for you, your department, and your school to rethink this curriculum. Changing your curriculum to a thematic and disciplinary integrated or interconnected curriculum will allow for much more flexibility with specific topics throughout your school year. Having a theme of "revolution" in a world history curriculum, for example, allows for a different learning approach, much greater integration, and much less pressure to cover massive amounts of information than does a curriculum that lists every revolution in history. Realistically, however, changing your curriculum is not always possible; it may be very difficult for you to let go of your familiar list of topics or your pet topic (e.g., "women in 20th-century Russia"); in fact, the school or department may not want to make the change. Whether you can or cannot change your curriculum, there is a way to introduce active learning approaches into your classes and still address all or most of your familiar topic areas.

Weaving Content Together

Creating a constructivist class is not about lowering standards or losing necessary content. It is not about students having to work less hard than in a traditional class. In fact, when you get back to the *real basics*, you will discover that the standards are higher, the content is more in-depth, student work is more involved and intense, and student learning is much more comprehensive. There is, however, a problem for many teachers and students in working in a thematic approach and leaving sequential formats behind. What you can do in this case is to become a weaver in your classroom.

Students Choose and Investigate Topics

Provide students with the list of topics from your curriculum content list and ask them to choose one of the topics, for either group or individual investigation. When they are ready, students will create and conduct a learning experience for the class based on their investigation of that particular topic. Students in the class will have to realize that what their peers do as they conduct a learning experience is as important as what the teacher does and that all students will be responsible for learning and understanding through these learning experiences. You can schedule these topics as you usually would, but it will be students who will involve other students actively in learning about their topic. This could include problem solving, role-playing, discussing, debating, creating questions, or any other active involvement. Will this happen overnight? Probably not. Will it be successful right away? Probably not.

You as a Weaver

The idea is not to let students flounder or conduct inadequate learning experiences for the class. You will monitor the ongoing work, intervene, and provide either direct instruction or provoking questions when necessary, either to students working on investigations or to the whole class if you think the learning experience missed important points. If some topics are missing altogether, you will be responsible for those. Your class will be a true collaboration of students and teacher; you will be using active learning approaches and addressing the content you want and feel obliged to address.

The Final Preparations for
Getting Back to the *Real Basics*

At this point, we are almost ready to look at a few specific active learning models. We will leave the content issue here by saying that you can use this weaving concept in any of the models we present in this chapter and at any grade level.

There are two things left to do before you implement the models. First, we will review Gardner's (1993) idea of multiple intelligences (MI) to provide a frame for the models; then we will look at how to make sure students, parents, and administrators understand the changes that will occur when you implement the models and why you are making these changes.

Multiple Intelligences: A Fable,
a Table, and Why We Shouldn't Label

A Modern Fable

One day, a special education professor was asked to do an educational evaluation of a 10th-grade student named Sam, who was described simply as a "behavior problem." Sam's school struggles began in the 1st grade. Since that time, he had been labeled as learning disabled, mentally retarded, emotionally disturbed, and language impaired, depending on the year he was tested and the person who did the testing. By the time Sam had reached the 10th grade, he refused to go to school and began receiving home tutoring from a man named Mr. Smith.

Mr. Smith reported that Sam was able to do a great deal more than he was led to believe, by school personnel, that Sam could do. He spoke at length about Sam's knack for fixing virtually anything mechanical (including car engines, grandfather clocks, and electric kitchen ranges), his strong ability to draw, and his memory for exactly how things looked long after he had seen them. Mr. Smith noted that Sam had difficulty expressing himself, read and wrote at about the 6th-grade level, and was extremely anxious and self-conscious about his weak academic skills. Although the primary focus of Mr. Smith's work was on helping Sam to obtain his driver's license, he indicated that he had successfully introduced academics "through the back door." For example, Mr. Smith had structured math and physics lessons around ice fishing trips and other outdoor activities, brought car manuals to Sam's house that they read together, and communicated in writing on the computer, frequently sending e-mail messages to one another about interesting engineering and mechanically oriented Web sites.

When the special education professor agreed to see Sam at his home office, he found Sam to be a polite, personable, and engaging adolescent. Although Sam was somewhat slow to warm up, after a brief walk outdoors and some tinkering with an old car parked at the professor's house, Sam initiated conversation easily, and rapport was established quickly. Sam struggled markedly on tests of reading and writing and on virtually all the evaluation measures that required fluent speaking skill, but he performed extremely well on measures that demanded mechanical problem solving, such as jigsaw puzzles and block designs. Sam shared with the examiner his love of cars, information about his collection of small engines, and a small portfolio of sketches he had made of various sorts of machinery. When asked about school, Sam became sullen. He noted that teachers only asked him to do "stuff I can't." He said that students frequently teased him, that he often became so frustrated that he got involved in fights, and that he hated school and would never return.

The teachers at school were happy that Sam was receiving home tutoring—they were happy that he was no longer their problem. Most believed he was headed for the criminal justice system; others noted that it was just as well. Sam, after all, was not very bright, and he had an attitude problem to boot.

Do you know Sam? What is so sad about this fable is that it is not fiction, not for Sam and not for others like him whose gifts lie outside what we for too long have considered to be intelligence. What is most striking about Sam, and about so many students in our schools, is what powerful learners they can be and what enormous talents they possess. To recognize these talents, we must look beyond our limited conception that to be intelligent and to learn, one must have strong verbal and/or logical-mathematical ability. Let's look more closely at an alternative way of thinking about intelligence, then return to Sam at the end of this section.

A Table: Expanding Our Cognitive Horizons

Howard Gardner's *Frames of Mind: The Theory of Multiple Intelligences* (1983) indicates that there are at least seven, perhaps more, distinct types of human intelligences. Although he was not the first to theorize that intelligence comes in many forms, Gardner has written extensively on the ways in which an understanding of multiple intelligences, or MI, can be applied in educational settings. A few model schools around the country are demonstrating how powerful this approach can be. At the Middle School of the Kennebunks, in Kennebunk, Maine, for example, students work in collaborative groups of seven, each representing one of the seven intelligences Gardner identified (see Table 5.1). At the Key School in Indianapolis, Indiana, students take traditional academic subjects but also have *daily* opportunity to develop their other intelligences in art, physical education, music, computer science, and foreign languages. Beginning in kindergarten, every student learns to play a musical instrument. At the Fuller School in Gloucester, Massachusetts, Julie Carter's 1st- and 2nd-grade MI classroom began the year by creating learning centers that serve as places where students can visit and design work focused on being "word smart," "math smart," "music smart," "people smart," and so on, focusing on one type of intelligence (Kugelmass, 1995).

In other schools around the country that have adopted MI approaches, a variety of common administrative and curricular features recommended by Gardner have been put in place. These include having

- assessment specialists, who are responsible for keeping a record of each student's learning and development in each of the seven areas;
- student-curriculum brokers, who seek to match available school resources (course electives, personnel, materials) with student interests and intellectual proclivities;
- school-curriculum brokers, who seek to match community resources with student needs;
- schoolwide themes, which organize curricula, sometimes at the level of an entire school;

- collaborative groups, composed of students who represent each of the seven intelligences; and
- pods, a type of learning group composed of students with similar interests and talents led by a teacher who serves as a mentor in an apprenticeship-like setting (Gardner, 1993).

Gardner believes that intelligence takes at least the seven different and independent forms shown in Table 5.1.

How to Label: One Intelligence or Many?

When we think of students who are doing poorly in our classrooms, we typically focus on the things they cannot do, or we speculate about the kinds of difficulty we believe may account for their weak school performance. The MI theory allows us to reframe our thinking about student performance. It calls on us to consider what our students do well, how they learn, and what they find intrinsically interesting so that we may label their strengths, as opposed to their weaknesses.

Let's return for a minute to our fable. Sam has always done poorly in school. Given what we know about him, would you say it is because he lacks intelligence? Are there things Sam does well? Could you think of a way that Sam could have shone in your classroom? Or do you think simply that school should not be for kids like Sam? How do we want to label students like Sam—by what they can do, or what they cannot do?

Preparing Students, Parents, and Administrators

Students and Parents

When you are ready to begin making changes in your classroom, you can handle the explanations for the students during class. These may take any of several forms but need especially to emphasize that the changes do not mean less work, or abandonment of behavior guidelines in the class, or lessening of standards, or that you are giving up your responsibilities. For parents, communication is essential. They will need written explanation of changes and how these will relate to content topics, standards, and grade formats. Without this clear explanation and reassurance that students will not lose but

TABLE 5.1 Types of Human Intelligences

Intelligence	Learner's Strengths
Intrapersonal	Ability to know self; ability to understand one's own strengths/weaknesses and motivations
Interpersonal	Ability to know others; ability to "read" social and/or political situations; ability to influence others; ability to lead and/or care for others—to be sensitive to needs of others
Bodily-kinesthetic	Ability to control the movement of one's body; ability to move in graceful, highly coordinated fashion
Musical	Ability to produce, write, and/or appreciate music
Spatial	Ability to shape, perceive, design, and/or conceive visual-spatial information; ability to remember visual information
Logical-mathematical	Ability to manipulate numbers and symbolic information; ability to draw logical conclusions; ability to think abstractly
Verbal-linguistic	Ability to manipulate, create, and appreciate the rhythms of language; ability to speak, read, and/or write fluently

rather will gain in their content and skill learning, you will have an ongoing problem on your hands.

Getting Your Principal on Board

The last thing you want to do is alienate your principal. How can you approach the principal so that she is there to support and encourage what you are doing? We surveyed principals all over the country in the three grade groupings—elementary, middle, and high school—and received back questionnaires from principals from the following states: New Hampshire, Vermont, Massachusetts, Washington, New Mexico, and Maine. Although we can't generalize from this small informal survey, we can say that these principals want and need their teachers to

- speak with them first—arrange a meeting to talk about ideas, obstacles, and concerns;
- be clear about their goals;
- think about how what they will do may affect their colleagues and be prepared for fallout;
- think about how they will respond to parental concerns;
- develop, research (including making school visits), and pilot test their ideas first, preferably within a team or at least with one other colleague;
- be clear about how they will assess learning;
- have clear expectations;
- go slowly; and
- demonstrate success *before* they become an apostle or complain about traditional methods.

Additionally, these principals give the following advice: Time is crucial; don't waste it. Be ready with a clearly written or oral plan, be ready with supporting evidence, and keep the principal advised on progress or concerns.

When All Else Fails

Although we advocate cooperation with school administrators, it is clear from our experiences—and perhaps your own—that there are times when you will need to go into your classroom, shut the door, and try something you are really convinced will work. We warn you that doing so could be detrimental to your job and general well-being. You can judge this for yourself. If your approach works, tell everyone; if it bombs, tell no one.

Are You Ready?

Run through Checklist 5.2 and see if you are ready to begin.

Tough Questions

1. Are certain "intelligences" more important for students to develop than others?

CHECKLIST 5.2

Preparation Checklist	*Yes*	*No*
I have explained to students why we will be making changes.	———	———
I have explained to students what the changes will be.	———	———
I have explained that changes do not mean students can do anything they want.	———	———
I have explained how student/teacher roles will be different.	———	———
I have written an explanation to parents explaining these changes.	———	———
I have met with the princiapl and explained what I will be doing.	———	———

2. How do you continue to encourage democratic classroom reform in the face of school board or parent pressure to use a regimented punishment-and-reward system of discipline?
3. What do you say to parents who believe grades and standardized testing are the only way they will be convinced that their child is learning?
4. How can you respond to parents who want less cooperative group work and more teacher dispensing of information, or who are concerned that their child is doing all of or not enough of the work?
5. Do all students need to learn to read and write? Why? Why not?
6. How can you assure parents that students are learning not only what they, the parents, think is necessary, but much more?
7. Do you have to become a subversive teacher to accomplish changes? Why? Why not?
8. How do you get over your own feeling that the "less is more" idea is too narrow a focus and will result in fragmented learning?

Six

Getting Your Feet Wet

If you have looked over the checklists and have made the necessary explanations and preparations with your students, your colleagues, parents, and administrators, you are ready to get your feet wet. We need to clarify here that there are hundreds of models of active learning that you can try. It is even better when you invent your own models. Remember that if you have not yet made the shift from emphasizing your teaching to emphasizing how students learn, none of these will work very well for you or the students. This chapter will outline three models: Where Is the Content?, Group Investigation, and National History Day. Remember, there is *no one road map*.

Where Is the Content?

Origin and Development of the Model

We call the first model "Where Is the Content?" It is based on the experiences and approach of Eliot Wigginton, founder of *Foxfire*, which began as a magazine—written and produced by students—about the oral history of Appalachian people. When Wigginton first started to teach secondary English at a conservative, semiprivate high school in Rabun Gap, Georgia, he found the students to be rebellious, indifferent, and perhaps even somewhat dangerous (e.g., they set his lectern on fire when he was lecturing). Realizing that his traditional methods were not working, he asked the students for suggestions of better ways to teach English. (Look at Chapter 10 to see how Susan used this approach.) The result was *Foxfire*.

Students interviewed local people and wrote about what they had learned. Cultural heritage became the motivating force for learning basic skills. Wigginton assumed that because the students were actively learning and not passively receiving, because there was an audience outside the classroom, and because the work flowed from the students' own interests and represented high standards, the students were learning English content and skills. He found support for his efforts when, in the early 1980s, John Puckett spent a year studying the *Foxfire* program (Puckett, 1986). Through a study of primary and secondary documents, observations, and interviews, Puckett found that compared to results from the boring and ineffective education described by Goodlad (1984) and Sizer (1984), *Foxfire*'s accomplishments were extraordinary, especially in its community/school relationships and in providing students with the opportunity to make decisions and to conduct their own learning.

At about the same time, however, Wigginton began to receive letters of dismay from teachers whose Foxfire programs were not working. These letters led Wigginton to look more closely at his program goals and results. After much reflection, Wigginton realized that producing a magazine had become the main goal for his classes, and publication deadlines had become more important than the educational process. In testing his students, he discovered (Puckett, 1989; Wigginton, 1985) that some knew no more about writing at the end of the year than they had at the beginning, though they had become excellent technicians.

This experience provides an important message for all teachers wanting to try new approaches. Although process skills such as collaborative editing, interviewing, and inquiry are important, they are not enough. Curriculum content is critical. As we noted in Chapter 5, saying that "the process is the content" is silly and simplistic. Although the *Foxfire* model now involves not only writing for magazines but also creating television shows, compact discs, and videotapes, there is a crucial new attention to state and school content objectives in the program.

The Model Steps

To make sure that you and your students meet both content and skill objectives of your curriculum while implementing an active learning approach, try the following.

1. Put content and skill objectives on a board, flip chart, or over-head. Take these objectives from your curriculum if you have one; if not, develop your own objectives.

2. Start with a very small project. For example:

   • Content objective: Students will be able to explain where Saudi Arabia is.

   • Skill objective: Students will demonstrate understanding of latitude and longitude.

3. Have students brainstorm instructional activities they think will accomplish these objectives.

   • You could put ideas on a board, flip chart, or overhead.

   • This exercise will allow students to get started with making choices and decisions about their own learning.

4. Review the activities with students.

   • Do not hand this over to students at this point. If they are not accustomed to doing this, chaos will result. If the students are used to you calling all the shots, keep them safe at this point.

   • Explain to them, or ask them (depends on your and their comfort level), which activities are possible and which are not, and why. This is not the time for students to be shouting out answers; keep it orderly. Either they can write down what they think or you can call on them one at a time.

5. Once you have a list of possible activities, have students reach agreement on the activities in which the class will engage.

6. Lead and oversee the activities and inform students that you will be doing this.

7. Evaluate learning: Did students demonstrate understanding of the content and ability to apply the skill?

This is a teacher-directed model with student input embedded in the framework. It is the beginning of students learning to be responsible for their own learning. They will have to learn which activities are possible and which are not. Remember, this is not about letting them do whatever they suggest: You have to use common sense here.

Group Investigation

The Basic Model

This model is based on methods proposed by Sharan and Sharan (1989/1990). As explained in Chapter 2, many cooperative learning methods focus on low-level skills and are simply traditional formats used with groups of students. Group Investigation (hereafter referred to as GI) focuses on academic achievement and on the development of higher-level thinking skills. This is a group project format in which students work in small groups and gather, analyze, and evaluate data and draw conclusions on a topic of their choosing. They then prepare a report and demonstrate their learning to the class. Peers and teachers evaluate the work.

Research on GI

Research (Sharan & Sharan, 1989/1990, 1992) that compares students in GI classes with those in traditional classes demonstrates that GI students in elementary and secondary schools have a higher level of academic achievement than students in traditional classes. The GI students also do better on questions assessing higher-level learning, although sometimes only just as well on acquiring information. On tests of social interaction, the traditional teaching methods stimulated a great deal of competition among students, whereas the GI method promoted cooperation, mutual assistance, and social interaction among classmates from different ethnic groups.

The Model Steps

Before you get into the steps, you probably will want to have a theme or question on which the class will be working. If the theme or question is part of your curriculum requirements, you do not have to worry about anyone questioning you about where the content is.

1. The group decides the topics to be explored.
   a. Students brainstorm possible subtopics/subquestions related to the larger theme or question. Questions work the best, but they have to be critical questions—how or why questions—that require and lead to substantial investigation.

   b. Students sort the subtopics/subquestions into categories.

   c. Students form groups by subtopics. If the investigation is at the beginning of the year and you don't know the students very well, a random group selection probably is the best method to use. If you know the students well, you can select the groups according to what you believe will be the most successful organizations. If you feel very brave and have worked with groups in this way before, you might try having the students select their own group members. This is the most likely method to fail, so save it for when you are feeling very confident about the method and the students.

2. The groups plan how they will investigate their subtopics or questions. This requires much work on your part. Students need to give you explicit details about how they will conduct their investigation. Students also need to give you explicit details on what each student in the group will be doing and how that will be different from what the others in the group will be doing. If you want this to *fail*, accept the following statements from the students:

- We are going to use the Web.
- Susie is going to read journals.
- Brian is going to do interviews.
- Adam will be reading newspapers.

If you want this to *succeed*, accept the following from the students:

- Susie is going to read the first chapter of *Future Shock* by Alvin Toffler by Tuesday, March 21.
- Brian is going to call Random House Publishers at 1-800-655-3456 on Tuesday using the phone in the guidance counselor's office and ask how to get in contact with Alvin Toffler. When he finds out this information, he will call Toffler and ask the following (attached) questions.
- Adam is going to interview Mr. Conklin and Ms. Boyce on Monday, March 20. This is already set up. The interview questions are attached.
- Melissa is going to the school library on Monday afternoon at 3 p.m. and will use the *New York Times Index* to find articles on Alvin Toffler and his book *Future Shock*.

Once the students have very explicit tasks, you move to the next step, but it is your responsibility to see that these tasks will be productive, possible, and explicit. You may need to have students create additional investigation tasks after they have completed the first tasks.

3. Students carry out tasks. Here you need to keep a check on the tasks and their completion. Students need to complete all tasks before moving ahead, and they need to provide you with detailed descriptions of how they will demonstrate task completion. For example:

   • Susie will give you a written summary of the chapter she has read and explain in writing what she has learned (not what she has learned about).

   • Brian will give you a written report of his phone conversation with Toffler or a written report of why it couldn't happen.

   • Adam will give you a written report of his interviews. He will give the responses and then draw conclusions.

   • Melissa will give you a written report of what she found in the *New York Times*.

4. Students plan a class learning experience based on their findings (once you are confident the students have done a thorough investigation). Here the details have to be as explicit as they were for the task descriptions. Who will do what? What will be the main experience: a debate? role-playing? a simulation? What will this look like?

5. The students conduct their learning experiences, which should demonstrate their understanding; peers will give feedback to students. Feedback could look like this:

   • The best thing about this learning experience was ___.

   • What I would like to see changed is ___ because ___.

6. Students and you evaluate the investigation and each individual's work and input. Here you can refer back to the section on assessment. Although the evaluation is the last step here, you should decide what form the assessment will take before you begin the GI process.

National History Day

Background of Model

If you have survived the first two models, you may be ready for more extensive active learning projects and more time-intensive work on the part of the students. If so, then the National History Day model (NHD) is for you. Although NHD is a national program related to the teaching and learning of history, you can adapt it to any subject area and any grade level. Active learning propositions provide the underpinnings for this program, which promotes student competency and interest in carrying out original research in history (this could be in any area) while improving student achievement and critical thinking skills.

More than 500,000 students across the United States participate in this program every year. Students in grades 4-12 select a topic related to an annual theme; find, analyze, interpret, and organize data; relate the data to a historical context; and develop a presentation on that topic in one of four formats: written research paper, group or individual tabletop project, group or individual media presentation, or group or individual performance. Students also must prepare an annotated bibliography of primary and secondary sources and write a one- to two-page description of how they researched and developed their presentation and of how their topic relates to the theme. In the official program, the program lasts from 6-9 months, depending on how successful the students are at district and state judging (the focus of which is to help students improve their entries). The program culminates in state winners participating at the national level in June at the University of Maryland. Historians, educators, and experienced professionals in related fields judge the entries.

Research on National History Day

A comprehensive study of this program (Page, 1992) suggests the following:

- National History Day provides a method of teaching and learning history that is superior to traditional methods.

- Through participation in the National History Day processes, students
  - Learn content, develop in-depth comprehension and awareness of issues, and gain transferable, lifelong skills
  - Gain self-confidence and self-esteem
  - Gain mastery and a feeling of competence
  - Gain a sense of who they are in relation to others
  - Learn the importance of group and team work and develop cooperative skills

The Steps

The first thing you need to ask yourself is this: Do you want your process to include judging, as the national program does? This would require that you ask people who have expertise in the area of students' investigations to be judges of the final products. This provides one way to encourage community involvement. You also will have to set up judging criteria. This process could be your assessment approach. It is important to note that the judging process in NHD not only allows judges and students to determine the level of analysis and understanding demonstrated through the project but also provides students with suggestions for improving their projects. At each level of judging, again except for the final judging at the national program, students are encouraged and expected to make changes in their work. The idea is that learning is not static but vibrant and ongoing. Once you have decided on whether to include this judging component, you can begin. Here are the steps to the model.

1. You alone or you and students select a broad theme or topic. If you or the community or the administration are worried about content, then this theme should be a topic out of your curriculum, especially for your first try at this. Themes that you could use in any content area would be something like
   - Rights and Responsibilities
   - The Individual in Society
   - Conflict and Compromise
   - Triumph and Tragedy

Or you could choose something that might be the title of a section in your textbook or out of your curriculum:

- Light
- Immigration
- Percentages
- Metaphors
- Neighborhoods

Or you could choose something very limited so that this project would be small. As small as you might think a project is, a project can take on a life of its own.

2. Clarify/define content and skill objectives as in the "Where Is the Content?" model.

3. Students and you define subtopics or subquestions as in the GI model. Students can brainstorm possible subtopics/questions and then come to agreement on five or six of the most promising. Possible subtopics might be

- What were the rights and responsibilities of the Irish immigrants in the early 1900s?
- What are the rights and responsibilities of pharmaceutical companies in developing new drugs?
- How can metaphors be used to define conflict?

4. Students form groups (or work as individuals). Use judgment again. If you are new at this and students are going to be working in groups, you decide group memberships; if you have a great deal of experience, do what works best for you.

5. Students in groups discuss how to investigate the issue or subtopic, and each group member defines his/her tasks. Step 2 of the GI model applies here, regarding students' plans for how to investigate their topic and specific tasks to be performed. If these task definitions are not explicit, this procedure will fail. For example, if the theme were immigration, promising task definitions might include the following:

- Jared will go to the school library tomorrow afternoon to find articles from the *New York Times Index* for 1920.
- Sean will interview his grandfather, an immigrant from Ireland, on Tuesday night.

- Sheila will go on Wednesday to the school library, set up the copy stand, and take photos from the *National Geographic* issue on immigration from February 1918.

6. Students decide what presentation format they will use for the final product. As explained briefly above, in the National History Day model there are four possibilities for how students will demonstrate their understanding and analysis of their topic:

   - Written paper—only individuals can select this.

   - Group or individual live performance—this requires doing the research; writing a script that demonstrates understanding, analysis, and mastery of the topic; and performing the script in 10 minutes or less.

   - Group or individual media production—this requires the same kind of research, writing a script, and then developing a media production that demonstrates understanding, analysis, and mastery of topic. The media presentation cannot be longer than 10 minutes. This time limit requires students to condense, synthesize, and demonstrate understanding of the most important concepts. The possibilities are endless and include drawings on overheads with analysis on audio tape, a slide show with audio tape analysis, a videotape production, a computer-aided demonstration, and Internet possibilities.

   - Group or individual tabletop project—requires same as above except that students demonstrate analysis and understanding through a stand-up project with specific size and word limitations: no taller than 6 feet, no wider than 40 inches, and no deeper than 30 inches (National History Day, Inc., 1986).

7. Students conduct the research/investigation. The scope of the project determines how long this will take: as little as one class period in your school or as long as the school year.

8. Check and recheck. This is where you monitor the reports from students on their investigation tasks. This is ongoing and allows you and the students to progress in a productive direction.

9. Students prepare an annotated bibliography of their work. (Yes, students in the 3rd grade can do this.) A workable model for all grades is to list bibliographical entries, with each entry followed by two sentences. The first sentence explains the content of the source. The second sentence explains how it was of value (specifically) in this research (i.e., "We used this source to determine percentages of Irish immigrants landing in the port of Boston on July 15, 1909.").

10. Students compile, interpret, and synthesize their material (photos, scripts, etc.).

11. Students prepare the demonstration and write a one- to two-page report per group on
    - how their subtopic relates to the theme;
    - how they conducted the research; and
    - how they developed the demonstration/product.

12. Students demonstrate their understanding, skills, and product.

Judging Format

If you have decided to use the judging format, here are some guidelines you might want to follow.

Judging

1. Select three judges.

2. Judges review each annotated bibliography and then ask students questions about their product/demonstration (5 minutes maximum, because the product should be able to stand alone). This conversation is to determine if students have done the research themselves and understand the concepts and significance of the topic.

Scoring

1. 60% of Score: Content Quality
   - Is the content accurate?
   - Is there analysis/interpretation of content rather than just a description?

- Do the students demonstrate understanding?
- Does the annotated bibliography demonstrate wide use of available sources?
- Were primary sources used?

Questions judges could ask to help determine score:

- What was your most important source and why?
- Why did you choose this category for your topic?
- What is the most important point you are trying to convey about your topic?
- What is the most important thing that you learned from completing this project?

2. 20% of Score: Demonstration Quality

- Is the entry original, creative, and imaginative in subject and implementation?
- Is all written material clear, grammatically correct, and correctly spelled?
- Does content display a measure of literary style?
- Is all visual material clear and appropriate?
- Do students display adequate familiarity with their equipment?
- Is acting of accomplished quality?

3. 20% of Score: Adherence to Theme and Rules

- Does the project focus on the theme/main topic?
- Does the project demonstrate the significance of the subtopic in relation to theme/main topic?
- Is the theme handled in a unique way?
- Did students operate all equipment?
- Did students create all parts of the project?
- Did students complete the demonstration in 10 minutes or less? (Automatic 5-point deduction if not.)

Tabletop projects do not have time limits but have size limitations: The project cannot be taller than 6 feet, wider than 40 inches, or deeper than 30 inches (National History Day, Inc., 1986, pp. 12-13).

Teacher Reflection

Each time you implement one of these models, you need to reflect on successes and problems. This will allow you to make adjustments for your classes for the next time you implement a model. Checklist 6.1 is a Reflection Checklist that is self-explanatory. It would probably be most useful if you stick with one model until most of your responses are in the "Yes" column.

Although some readers may want to stick to these models for a while, others with more teaching experience may be ready for more complex constructivist approaches. In the next chapter, we discuss issues pertinent to the various grade levels and present teachers who describe models—including interdisciplinary team investigations, student-developed curricula, and theme-based programs—that are more constructivist in nature than those described in this chapter. These teachers will introduce you to their procedures, successes, and concerns.

Tough Questions

1. If students make choices as to what they investigate, how can you ensure that there is any unifying thread in your classroom?

2. How can you use these models in sequential subject areas such as math and foreign languages?

3. How will you handle parents who say that this is way too much work and is interfering with family life?

4. How will you make sure student groups have the same opportunity for investigation and product development in terms of equipment and material they need?

5. How will you handle parents who try to do part of the students' work on these projects?

6. How will you set up and explain assessment tools for these kinds of approaches?

7. How will you determine if implementing these models has made any difference in learning for your students?

CHECKLIST 6.1

Reflection	First Time		Second Time		Third Time	
	Yes	*No*	*Yes*	*No*	*Yes*	*No*
Students were totally involved.	——	——	——	——	——	——
Students understood what they were doing and why.	——	——	——	——	——	——
Students liked the new approach.	——	——	——	——	——	——
Students were able to demonstrate under-standing.	——	——	——	——	——	——
Students' understanding of content was superior.	——	——	——	——	——	——
I felt comfortable doing this.	——	——	——	——	——	——
This was the hardest thing I've ever done.	——	——	——	——	——	——
I want to do this again.	——	——	——	——	——	——
I was thrilled by the students' engagement.	——	——	——	——	——	——
I was organized and clear about what I was doing.	——	——	——	——	——	——
I saw tremendous im-provement in students' work and comprehension.	——	——	——	——	——	——

8. A new teacher, Dave Antonio, introduced the National History Day model to his high school biology class. The theme was composting. There was a requirement that students demonstrate understanding of composting through some form of technology. Dave explained, "While their projects were extremely diverse, the students spent more time learning about technology than about composting. This was valuable, but I felt they lost the focus of the topic." What would you do to avoid this happening in your class?

9. When Rachel Marsh introduced Group Investigation processes to her 6th-grade students, they seemed excited. The students, however, did not seem able to work cooperatively in groups. What would you do to prepare students for the Group Investigation processes to avoid this problem?

10. What issues are generated for you when, after a constructivist investigation, students submit their work to be judged?

Seven

Diving In
Teachers Tell Their Stories

We were studying ancient Greece. Students had researched a particular person of the time and came prepared to enter into dialogue as that person. One minute before class, my department chairperson, who had been hearing all of these stories about my unorthodoxy, announced that he was going to sit in on the class. So we began. The students really got into it as I asked Alcibiades and Zeno and Aristotle what they thought about various topics and about the comments of Socrates. Students were going crazy, jumping in with comments and questions, while staying in their roles. After class, I got no comment from the Chair, so I asked him for a reaction. "You've got some very good students there. You do teach the political facts, though, don't you?" he replied. (D. Christensen, personal communication, January 31, 1997)

How do real teachers get back to the *real basics*? How do they set up classrooms to allow for and encourage active learning? How do they handle the unique challenges that constructivist classrooms and their grade levels present? How do they deal with administrators, parents, school board members, and other teachers who simply don't get it? In this chapter, you will meet teachers at the elementary, middle, and secondary levels, and you will hear what they have done, what challenges they face and have faced, and what issues they have had to address. More important, you will see how they have developed their own styles and models for creating and sustaining their constructivist classrooms. Each of the following sections begins with issues relevant to the grade level.

Leaving Home for the
Bigger World (Grades K-4)

A primary issue for elementary teachers is how to develop experiences that will allow our youngest students, many of whom have not yet cut their second set of teeth, to interact with, integrate, and understand what seems like vast amounts of new information. For many of these teachers, interdisciplinary approaches that emphasize student-directed, active learning are old hat. For too many others, blending science and art, math and English, and other arbitrary subject areas could not be more foreign. When we visit local elementary schools, we are often struck by the number of teachers who use lecterns(!); who spend more time talking, telling, and instructing than listening, guiding, and facilitating learning; and who break content learning into regimented time blocks as if, for example, students could only learn math between 9:10 and 9:42. On one recent visit, we observed a 3rd-grade classroom in which the teacher's blackboard contained the following information:

Spelling—8:12-8:37
Language Arts—8:37-9:02
Reading—9:02-9:27 . . .

We didn't read to the bottom of the board: The first three lines were perfectly clear. In this room, the teacher views and introduces even closely related subjects as separate from one another; the teacher presents new information every day, in the same order, in the same way.

As noted in Chapter 5, the way one views the curriculum drives teaching and learning. If you view language arts, spelling, and reading as distinct from one another, you will tend to convert opportunities for the *learning* of language, spelling, or reading into preset time schedules for the *teaching* of language, spelling, or reading. Even if you don't think this way, administrators often make the kinds of curriculum decisions that require you to break *learning* into *teaching* segments. Many teachers feel compelled to follow along. If you want to implement constructivist approaches in such an elementary classroom, you *will* need to address this issue. The teacher you are about to meet describes quite a different approach to student learning.

Meet Jan Carpenter

"Jan Carpenter" (a pseudonym), is an experienced teacher in a multiage 2-3 classroom in a community of lower socioeconomic level outside Burlington, Vermont. Jan took some of the core ideas from the whole language reading approach and used them as a foundation for drastic changes in her teaching of disciplinary content. As you read Jan's story, think about the whole language emphasis on integrating learning experiences, on the use of journals, and on the sharing of learning with others.

Jan's Mind Shift

Several years ago, after teaching for 13 years, I began gradually to change the way I perceived children as learners. It happened because of my introduction to the whole language philosophy. Instead of looking at children as glasses waiting to be filled, I saw them as fires waiting to be ignited. I realized that children were naturally curious about the world around them and were constantly formulating ideas to explain their discoveries. And I came to see that if they had meaningful and interesting activities with enough time for exploration and validation they would develop true understanding. While a traditional approach often suited my needs as a teacher, it did little for my students.

Along with the whole language philosophy, what had the most profound impact on my teaching approach was participation in the Vermont Elementary Science Project. This gave me opportunities to experience inquiry science. I learned how to collect, organize, analyze, test, and apply evidence. I knew this was the approach I wanted for my students. My role as teacher changed drastically. I became a facilitator. I no longer stood in front of the class disseminating information. I set up activities that would help build on students' prior knowledge or understanding of a concept. This approach, which started from student interest, not only connected the learning of science to whole language propositions but allowed me to integrate other subject areas in learning activities.

Jan's Process

Even though I was focused on science, I developed a program that integrated science, math, and language arts. Why? Two reasons: First, learning is not done in isolation; it's interconnected. For example, how can you possibly learn about light without figuring out angles? Second, integration provides the most precious gift a teacher can receive—time. It took a few years before my science, math, and language arts program truly reflected my beliefs. Here is my approach now.

First stage. In the first stage, I provide opportunities for students to become actively curious about our topic. I create this invitation in various ways: New objects to explore and to explore with, observations of the natural world, or a problem to be solved might promote active inquiry in this stage. Students start to ask: "What is this?" "What does it do?" "What do I already know about this?"

Second stage. In the next stage, students explore and discover. They begin by "messing around" with the materials. This focused play gets the students ready for more in-depth observations. Students can't make detailed observations until they've had an opportunity to engage in free exploration of materials. For example, if students have never seen or used a light box, you can't expect them initially to use it to gather information about light. Their fascination with it would prohibit these discoveries until they had time to explore its superficial features.

After students spend an appropriate amount of time exploring, a stimulating or productive question will create an invitation to take a closer look or to encourage a new investigation. These questions ask children to show rather than to say answers. Many begin with "How . . ." or "Why do you think. . . ." Throughout this phase, students are recording observations and ideas. Students are talking with each other. They are sharing, discussing, debating, and discovering.

To integrate technology into the learning, I present the following design technology challenges:

- *Design Technology Challenge #1: Build a functioning lighthouse that is at least 16 inches high and which allows light to be seen from all angles. (materials: poster board, wood from the linx kits, clear cups, glue, wire, flashlight bulbs, D batteries)*

- *Design Technology Challenge #2: Build the most inexpensive device that can be used to search for things lost in the dark. (materials: wood, poster board, Dixie cups, D batteries, flashlight bulbs, wire, tape)*

Third stage. The third stage involves students communicating their explanations and solutions. This reporting out time is similar to a scientific convention. Students present the evidence they have acquired during their investigations via charts, diagrams, and drawings. This gives students the opportunity to demonstrate their understanding of the concept or skill.

What If You Are Not Jan Carpenter?

Jan Carpenter, as explained above, is an experienced teacher and reached this level of success after 5 or 6 years of working with and adjusting the procedures and steps. The first time you try any constructivist approaches, you probably will have a mixture of successes and problems. This is why reflection is so essential at the end of each attempt. Each subsequent time you try the approach, you will have ironed out some of the things that didn't work. In the next section, after looking at the main issues at the middle school level, you will meet two middle level teachers who had much success in implementing a constructivist-based, student-developed curriculum but realized they would need to revise the process the next time around.

If You Don't Know/Remember What Young Adolescents Are About, You Will Wish You Did (Grades 5-8)

Young Adolescent Needs

Between the ages of 10 and 14, students will change more rapidly and pose more divergent issues for their teachers than at any other time in life except infancy. It is in these grades where we first begin to lose students to the educational system. According to *Turning Points*, the middle grades "are potentially society's most powerful force to recapture millions of youth adrift, and help every young person thrive during early adolescence" (Carnegie Council on Adolescent Development, 1989, p. 8). Although some students are beginning to make a transition from concrete reasoning to abstract thinking, most middle school students are still operating at a concrete thinking level. This means that they learn best when involved in a real problem. This fits with the concepts of constructivism—that is, that the longest-lasting and deepest learning occurs when it occurs in context.

Physically, middle grade students have as wide a range in development as in cognitive development. The young women can mature physically 2 years before the young men. Students may appear awkward or gawky and be very uncomfortable sitting for long periods of time because bone growth can exceed muscle development. Besides the cognitive and physical changes, there are emotional and social changes. The most crucial search of their lives—Who am I? How do I compare to others?—begins at this age. Friends and peer groups and belonging become increasingly important to young adolescents. These characteristics and needs drive everything else that happens in middle grade reform, and they need to be at the core of your constructivist approaches.

Teaming in the Block

Some of you probably are already familiar with organizational features recommended to enhance the learning experiences of middle schoolers. These features include interdisciplinary teaming and block scheduling. The rationale behind interdisciplinary teaming or partnering is that it allows teachers to work with each other in flexible time periods to best meet the learning needs of students as well as to get to know students better and to let students feel as if they belong. Block scheduling, which complements the interdisciplinary format, allows teachers in the team or partnership to decide, for example, that on a certain day the students need longer to investigate a science problem. This longer time period is meant to allow for, and support, the active learning approaches of constructivism. It also allows integration of subject matter. For example, on Monday students might spend a 2-hour block of time on science experiments, and on Tuesday they might spend a 2-hour block on solving math problems connected to the science experiments, or the math and science teachers on the team might work together for the total of 4 hours and integrate the material and tasks for both days. To get the most from your constructivist approaches, you will need to be familiar with the possibilities and requirements of block scheduling.

Christos, Ariel, and Their Classmates
Develop Their Own Curriculum

At the most progressive end of the constructivist continuum are the schools in which students not only construct their own knowledge through active learning processes but also play a major role in developing their own curriculum. Although this is not as common a component of middle schools as interdisciplinary teaming, for example, it will be to your advantage to understand the possibilities of this approach. Questions about the students and their world generate themes that students investigate throughout the year (Beane, 1993; Brodhagen, Weilbacher, & Beane, 1992). The investigations typically include all the major subject areas in an integrated fashion. At the Williston Central School of Williston, Vermont (Burrello, Burrello, & Winninger, 1995), which is probably one of the most progressive and most constructivist middle schools in the nation, students in multiage (grades 5-8) groupings not only define and develop much of their curriculum but also determine how, and to some extent when, they will conduct an investigation.

Christos's and Ariel's Parents/Guardians Need to Know

Keeping Track, Grading, and Communicating

Parents need to have clear explanations of how you and students keep track of their work; additionally, they can have major issues about grades and grading systems with which they have had no experience. An increasingly common grading practice at many middle schools that support constructivist propositions involves students developing the criteria for assessing their own work. At Williston Central School, students develop what are called Quality Indicators for every project or piece of work. When the indicators the students suggest are either not valid or simply are not attainable, the facilitator helps to redirect the students in developing more productive kinds of indicators. The more the students practice self-assessment with the facilitator's assistance and feedback, the sooner they become expert at evaluating their own work in relation to a high standard.

Whatever grading system you use, many parents will equate letter grades of A, B, C, D, and F to whatever terms or symbols you use, whether they mean similar things or not. Clear and frequent communication from you about students' progress is necessary and critical. Your work is not done simply because you send newsletters home at the beginning of the year or semester. This communication is necessary throughout the year and at all parent meetings.

Don't Forget the Content

Parents can get very concerned when they don't see evidence of, or can't find in their students' work, content topics. They will question how their children will be ready for high school if they are not addressing this content. They have every right to be concerned, not so much in relation to whether students will be prepared for high school (there are many things that need to change in the high schools) but because content is a major piece of education and learning. If you cannot show or explain where and what the content is and how it is not the same as the content of last year or the year before, something is wrong. You may be paying too much attention to the process and not enough to the "beef." This is so whether you are working alone or with team members in interdisciplinary approaches.

Meet Ann Lipsitt and Janette Roberts

Ann is a 7th- and 8th-grade special educator, and Janette is a language arts/social studies teacher in the 8th grade at Browns River Middle School, about 25 miles from Burlington, Vermont. A large percentage of the students at Browns River come from professional families. There are about 500 students in grades 5-8. Ann and Janette, who had recently completed a course that focused on instruction and curriculum in the middle grades, decided to involve their students in developing part of the curriculum. In this project, Ann and Janette tried to address the issue of young adolescent identity search, to incorporate recommended organizational features described above such as block scheduling and interdisciplinary partnering, and to involve the students in self-assessment.

Ann and Janette's Process

You're probably thinking the idea of student-developed curriculum—a process in which students generate questions about themselves and their world and then choose related themes to investigate—sounds nice, but how does it work really in a classroom of 24-25 students and on a middle school team. Our team includes 50 students, the two of us, and a variety of auxiliary personnel who assist with students with special issues or disabilities. The topic for our project was immigration and industrialization in the United States during the late 1800s to early 1900s, a time period mandated by the district's history curriculum.

Engaging the Students

To get our students actively involved in understanding the impact of industrialization and immigration on life in the 19th century, we did three things. First, we went to a local museum where each of us (yes, the students too) assumed a role typical of the time period. Everyone experienced life in the 1800s as a person living in a rural environment among an extended family. Students worked with farm animals, prepared a complete meal, performed household chores, quilted, and discussed issues of the times as they performed their jobs. Next, students wrote reaction papers which addressed how they felt about the experience and what they learned. And finally back in the classroom the students read at least one novel to extend their understanding of the time period and to broaden their interest of the topics they were studying.

Developing the Curriculum

After a week of reading, each student designed a character and assigned him/herself a role determining whether he/she would be a farmer, immigrant, mill worker, working child, or possibly an overseer. Each student developed a character and made up a life story for this person using the information he or she had learned. As students wrote about their characters, they also made lists of interests, problems, and questions they would have experienced and had in their daily lives. This not only engaged the students, but allowed them to tap into the deep issue of Who Am I? Their own issues came out through their characters' issues. From these lists of concerns, questions, and issues, the students developed broader topics or themes. Using large pieces of newsprint, we wrote their themes and topics down for future reference. These lists remained on the walls throughout this project. There were 14 themes/topics ranging from Irish immigration to labor reform.

Each student received a typed copy of the lists. Together, we generated specific questions we might want to answer about each topic/theme. We came up with a list of almost 50 questions. As the list grew, so did the students' interest. The questions included "How did immigration impact Americans?," "Why didn't everyone get the same education?," and "How was the world reacting to successes in America?"

Brainstorming Activities

After developing the questions, students brainstormed activities that could be used to find answers and other activities that could demonstrate their knowledge and understanding of the questions. It still delights us that the students created a list of possible activities that was uncannily similar to the one we created in anticipation of this process. For obtaining the information, the students came up with:

- *Inviting guest speakers to classroom*
- *Watching videos and documentaries*
- *Writing, calling, or using e-mail for information from Ellis Island, Sheldon Museum, Shelburne Museum, the Vermont Historical Society, local historical societies, and the Vermont Folklife Center*
- *Interviewing local people to obtain oral histories*
- *Using school, local college, and regional libraries*
- *Taking field trips to museums and local mills*
- *Researching local records at town offices*
- *Getting information from the World Wide Web*
- *Reading biographies and historical fiction*

And for demonstrating understanding and knowledge, they thought of:

- *Building a scale model*
- *Doing a painting or mural*
- *Making a collage*
- *Writing and performing a song*
- *Creating games*
- *Making puzzle books*
- *Writing a typical cookbook*
- *Preparing typical foods*

- *Making and demonstrating crafts*
- *Producing a video*
- *Creating a visual presentation*
- *Producing multimedia presentations*
- *Creating a music video*
- *Preparing wax museum pieces*
- *Writing and performing a skit or play*
- *Creating advertising brochures*
- *Making posters*
- *Teaching younger students*
- *Developing a simulation*
- *Role-playing*
- *Creating a time line*
- *Writing a newspaper*
- *Constructing a public display*
- *Preparing a flip book or pop-up book*
- *Writing a research paper*
- *Retelling stories of the time period*
- *Creating inventions using materials and tools of the time period*

Investigating

Next, students chose a topic for investigation. We asked a variety of questions to help students pick topics of interest to them. We made judgment calls about what were reasonable choices and productive learning experiences. Some ideas that kids came up with needed to be discarded or significantly revised. For example, one student decided she wanted to study women in the labor movement. Unfortunately, the topic became overwhelming and she found herself floundering among the information and the number of events that were occurring at that time. Through our questioning, she was able to narrow her topic to the Triangle Factory fire, which allowed her to study the women's movement within a particular framework.

Negotiating Assessment

Before the investigations began, together with the students we developed a rubric to define quality work. This was done fairly easily as the students had been working on rubric development all year. Students also observed and analyzed models of excellent and poor quality work so that they could under-stand what makes a product effective or ineffective. The students decided they wanted to share their work with a wider audience, so together we designed the culminating day to include historically accurate games, dressing up in time-period costumes, and creating a potluck meal. All of this was decided before the research began.

Working in Block Time

In addition to working outside of the classroom, students had 80-minute work periods three times a week for 3 weeks to do research and develop a project. At the end of each block time, students wrote a journal entry with the following specific items:

- *What did I accomplish?*
- *What resources did I use?*
- *What is my plan for the next scheduled block time?*
- *What materials do I need next?*
- *What problems am I having?*

All responses had to be detailed and specific. This was difficult for students who were not used to being specific, so we created a model of a detailed journal and made overheads of exemplary journal entries.

Results

Successes

We believe that the students learned more about this time period than we could ever have possibly "covered." Everyone learned to be a researcher, how to ask good leading questions, how to look at cause and effect relationships from a historical perspective, how to manage time, and how to organize and orchestrate a project from initial questions to conclusions. And most of all, everyone learned what living in the 19th century might have been like. They also developed a better understanding of how past events affect our lives today. Because they generated the questions and searched to find the answers to their own questions, we believe they are more likely to remember this learning experience. And, because so much of the investigation was done by the indi-vidual learners themselves, we believe that they have mastered many of the skills necessary for continuing to generate questions and to know how to locate answers and find solutions not only from textbooks and authority figures, but from a whole host of other sources as well.

When we asked students to reflect on this learning experience, almost all of them stated that they appreciated and liked having the opportunity to make choices about what to learn and how to demonstrate what they had learned. The most positive and numerous response was that they had had a lot of fun during the culminating day's activities.

Problems

Everything initially did not run smoothly. Lots of students needed guidance and direction. They wanted us to tell them what they should do, and it was tempting to give them our ideas. One of the biggest problems was knowing when and when not to intercede. For example, one group of self-directed students wanted to create a cookbook and menu—everyone would sign up and bring in a dish they had researched and determined appropriate to the time period. This sounded reasonable until we looked at the list of dishes they were selecting. We knew that few families would have the ingredients necessary to make some of the highly unusual ethnic dishes which they had selected. A compromise was finally reached when we agreed on a luncheon meal which included a variety of pastas and ethnically diverse desserts—typical dishes made by family members. The menu planners were unhappy with us and our interference with their plans. They felt we had given them the reins and then taken them back.

There were other problems as well. Some parents did not understand this model and didn't see the value in self-directed study. Additionally, we didn't always know what each of us on the team was doing and which students were getting assistance and which were falling through the cracks.

Reflections

The next time we would like to have students not working all the time with their project-mates, but to form other groups with students working on different projects. This would allow students to share ideas, problem solve, and brainstorm with—and offer suggestions to—students from other groups. The students could then take back some ideas to their project team.

The biggest change we would make, though, has to do with communication. First, we would communicate more about the model with parents; second, we would make changes in team communication. We could carry around clipboards *with a student roster. As we speak with students, we could keep a log for reference at team meetings. We could then decide who would meet with students with whom we had not interacted. This communication and coordination is essential. Without this, constructivist, active learning approaches may become disjointed, the curriculum pieces may no longer complement each other, and some students may feel lost.*

Student Boredom, Alienation, and the "Who Am I?" Question (Grades 9-12)

A main issue at the high school level involves the "Who am I?" question. There are some high school students—particularly those whose confidence and identity are connected to high grades—who feel comfortable in the traditional system. They have mastered the schooling game, know how to memorize and recite back, know what the teacher wants, and feel safe. There are millions of other teenagers, however, who are bored, disinterested, and disconnected. It would be a rare teenager who woke up shouting to the rooftops: "I can't wait to get to math class and do calculus!" or "I can't wait to get to Mr. Gotha's class so we can watch a video of the New Deal!" or "I can't wait to get to English today so I can practice grammar rules . . . AGAIN!" Typical adolescent lethargy is not only a result of boring teaching approaches but also a result of educators paying little attention to the developmental needs of their students. As with the emerging adolescents of the middle grades, high school students have priorities that often are unrelated to school (at least in traditional settings). Like middle schoolers, most are still asking, "Who am I?" In the traditional educational format, there is very little connection to this central question of identity.

From Adam to the Atom in 10 Months: Welcome to World History With Mr. Shoate

A second crucial issue at the high school level is that the curriculum is usually content driven. The problem here, as we discussed in Chapter 5, is that you can't separate curriculum from instructional approach, and if the high school curriculum is heavily weighted with lists of topics to be covered (as we suggest in the heading above), there is only one way for teachers to feel as if they are accomplishing what they are expected to do, and that is to provide direct instruction most of the time. This is especially true if teachers are still working in the traditional 40- or 50-minute time periods. Under pressure to *get to* World War II by the end of the year or to *get to* equations by January, teachers will deliver information as fast as they can and then move to the next topic. This approach does not allow for in-depth study or for ways for students to see connections among topics or disciplines or to see relevancy to their own lives.

Preparing for SATs and Other College Entrance Exams

A third issue you will ignore only at great peril is that of student preparation for the SATs and other college entrance exams. Whether they ought to be or not, these exams are a major concern for parents and teachers at the high school level. New teaching approaches, especially constructivist, interdisciplinary approaches that may not clearly define content areas, are especially problematic for parents and administrators who ask: Can active learning approaches, which focus on inquiry and depth of understanding rather than massive amounts of information, prepare students adequately for these exams? Although there is much research showing that constructive approaches lead to equal if not greater success in all academic areas (see Chapter 2), it is difficult to appease and convince parents and others with these reports. There are parents and students who will feel that time is being wasted, that the teachers are getting paid to teach (translate as "tell") and should be doing it, and that projects and activities may be entertaining but are essentially without substance and pointless. Even though we know (Clinchy, 1994; Conley, 1996) that standardized tests for the most part do not measure the depth of, or ability to apply, understanding; and even though we know that more and more colleges are eliminating or making an option of the SATs; and even though we know that these kinds of test scores are not the best predictors of success in either college or life, if you are trying to make changes in your classroom, you have to be aware of these parental/administrator worries and issues, and you need to address them head on.

Changing Times at Ridgemont High

In the Block

If you are a high school teacher who has not yet experienced block scheduling, you probably won't have to wait much longer. This change is happening everywhere—in some places through the actions of the administrators or teachers themselves and in other places through statewide efforts in educational reform. The rate of change to block scheduling in high schools is dramatic. Recent estimates are that at least 50% of American high schools have already changed, are currently studying how to change, or are in the process of changing to block scheduling (Canady & Rettig, 1996).

Why Block Scheduling?

It has long been known that 40- or 50-minute periods lead to fragmentation of learning. Think about this: Carlos is 15 years old in a traditional high school. He starts his first class at Pueblo High School at 7:45 a.m. In 40 minutes, the bell rings, and he switches gears not only in academic subjects but in classroom settings, processes, requirements, and dynamics for another 40 minutes. He does this seven or eight times a day. When he returns to the math class on the following day, after six or seven other 40-minute classes have disrupted that learning experience, he is expected to pick up where that class left off the day before. It is a disconnected, choppy curriculum at best, with few if any connections among subject areas made apparent to the students.

Block scheduling allows teachers to have, for example, 90 minutes to conduct learning experiences connected to material formerly addressed in a 40-minute period. This extra time will allow students to become actively engaged in more in-depth learning and comprehension. Unfortunately, many teachers do not know how to handle block scheduling and don't know why it is happening. Some just continue to use traditional approaches and move into the 90-minute period what they formerly did in two 40-minute periods. Not only is this not the purpose of block scheduling, it won't work. How many teenagers do you know who can remain alert for a 90-minute lecture?

Moving in and Around the Block

For experienced teachers used to traditional scheduling, this change can be very unnerving. It is only natural that an extended period would seem to be just more of the same, only more difficult. It should be neither. It should generate very different kinds of learning approaches. It is not only the teachers who have to get used to something new. You can't expect students to jump into a new environment or system without warning or gradual change. In particular, you cannot expect them to do this if the assessment process changes as well and moves from a *recite it back* mode to a *demonstration of understanding* format. This can be most unnerving to the "A" students who have spent a school lifetime mastering that traditional system and who suddenly feel as if they will lose their edge when other students, who are more willing to take risks (after all, their grades may already have been mostly mediocre), begin to shine.

Interdisciplinary Teaming in the Block

As with the elementary and middle grades, at many high schools there is a new emphasis on connecting and integrating curriculum and on working in teams (Clarke & Agne, 1997). Although this is often a difficult adjustment at the middle grades, at the high school, where content-driven departments feel a strong connection to and possession of their academic areas, this kind of change is a huge leap. Even if you are interested in and feel ready to shift to an interdisciplinary teaming approach, the person or persons who will be working with you on the team may not be anywhere near as ready and in fact may resent you and the changes. This is a good time to keep Susan Jackson's experience in mind. Tread slowly. These kinds of changes will require the same effort at communication as noted with efforts at the middle grades.

Students as Change Agents

Although local and national political groups may attempt to sidetrack these reforms, it is the students themselves who may be the fundamental change agents in the high schools. They now have access to information by phone, fax, e-mail, and the World Wide Web.

Teachers can't compete with these information supplies. Students crave finding more and more and want to know how to put it all together. Additionally, as students move up from reformed middle schools, they are demanding different approaches to, and clearer purposes for, their learning experiences at the high school.

Addressing It All

This is a lot to think about: adolescent boredom, the adolescents' quest to find their identity, pressure from jam-packed curricula lists, students who will resist changes, students who demand change, parents and administrators who are worried about standardized testing, and implications of block scheduling and interdisciplinary teaming for working conditions and professional relationships. As you introduce constructivist approaches, you need to be aware of and address these issues while keeping in mind that your main concern has to be student learning. As you read the following report of Katy Smith, see if you can determine how she addresses and has addressed these issues.

Meet Katy Smith

Katy Smith is an English teacher at Addison Trail High School in Addison, Illinois, and she will close this chapter for us. Her descriptions and dialogue bring together the issues, questions, concerns, and possibilities of constructivist approaches—at the high school level in particular and at all grade levels in general.

The Process for Katy Smith and Her
Teaching Partners Ralph Feese and Rob Hartwig:
Students Negotiate the Curriculum

Katy and Ralph, English and social studies teachers, respectively, first teamed to teach an 11th-grade American Studies Program, which focused on history and literature, during the 1988-1989 school year. In the fifth year of this program, students became actively engaged in developing the curriculum. As with Ann and Janette at the middle grades, Katy and Ralph asked students to brainstorm questions they felt needed to be answered about a particular topic and then asked them to suggest, select, and follow through on activities that would help them answer the questions. Katy and Ralph gave few traditional tests during the semester, and what tests they did give were interdisciplinary, not separate history or English tests. They assessed students mainly through their papers, projects, and presentations (Smith, 1993). The details of this project's procedures are much the same as Ann and Janette describe in the previous section (see Beane, 1993, and Brodhagen et al., 1992), so we won't elaborate on them here. Instead, we will listen to Katy reflecting on the last several years of working with the American Studies Program as well as with the Freshmen Studies Program that she and Ralph piloted with science teacher Rob Hartwig 4 years ago.

Reflections

The Process/Content Issue

There is no such thing as learning a process unless you're learning that process doing something with meaningful content. We've really struggled over the past few years to define that particular issue. It is essential that kids be involved in the processes that involve thinking, but you can't learn to think without having something to think about. You've got to have the content there. As part of an interdisciplinary situation, I've been forced and challenged to examine what is the really essential, really important content. I get a little nervous about people who talk about covering the content because to cover is to obscure. There has to be a balance. The critical question to ask yourself is why a particular topic is important.

Interdisciplinary Curriculum

In interdisciplinary contexts students can get to look at a problem through different lenses. Let me give you an example from our class that we teach together. This is called Freshmen Studies and includes English, social studies, and now science since Rob has joined our team. One of the projects in which we have been involved is the Illinois Rivers Project. Basically what we have done is adopt a portion of Salt Creek, which is a part of the Illinois River system. It's right in our community and takes us about 5 minutes by bus. Since we are teaming we have the first three periods of the day to schedule as a block.

The first time we took a trip out to the creek to plan what we wanted to do, we each found an angle that worked for us. Rob was really involved in water testing—getting the kids to take the samples to find out really specific bio-chemical kinds of things. Ralph had been doing some things with geographical features and talking about how meandering happens, how cut banks happen, how humans interact with the river. I had been looking at the river in terms of its symbolism and its power in literature and in music and how the experience of being on the river can inspire poetry and fiction.

Three Perspectives

Ralph had planned to do a geographical survey—to walk the kids up and down the creek and to have them look at the different elements—upstream, down-stream, etc. Rob was going to do water testing, and I thought of sitting and looking at the relationship between nature and humans and the environment and different points of view—in the creek, on the side of the creek. We got on the buses to go back to school and each of us looked like the cat who had swallowed the canary because each of us had gotten to do the things which dealt with important concepts connected to our disciplines and which we really enjoyed. But for the kids, it was an experience from three different perspec-tives. Some liked certain parts better than others, but everyone liked some part of the experience, and their follow-up work demonstrated a high level of learn-ing. Some kids got into writing letters to the water commission and the forest preserve district. Others said things like, "I never knew that forest preserve was there—that's a really great place to go."

Subsequent Trips to the River

A couple of times since then, we have had our math teacher join us. Math is not part of our block schedule at this time because the students are at such different levels of readiness and we haven't been able to figure out how to incorporate math on a full-time basis. But the math department chairperson came out to the creek with us and he did some things with the kids about how to measure the depth, how to determine the flow of the creek, and then he gave them a problem: If you knew the rate at which the creek was flowing, if the gymnasium was this big, how long would it take for the creek to fill up the gym? Again, kids said things like, "I hadn't ever considered any of these things. I hadn't ever looked at it in this way."

Becoming Your Own PR Person:
Addressing Concerns

SATs and College Preparation

We have been very aware of the concerns of parents and administrators in regard to student preparation for college in relation to our interdisciplinary and student-developed curriculum. We have been conducting follow-up studies to address this kind of concern. So far in the data, there is nothing to indicate that kids are not making appropriate academic progress. Illinois has a set of assessments that kids have to take at various points. The data our assessment center has gathered shows that the students in our program are doing as well as or slightly better than their peers. They certainly aren't going down. What we hear from teachers, for better or worse, is that these students have good questioning skills and know how to generate and identify problems and propose possible solutions. For example, at a recent in-service meeting, one of our social studies colleagues recently commented that he can tell in his classes which of the students who are now juniors and seniors came from our Freshmen Studies program because when it comes time to do library research, they are the ones to say, "Oh, OK" and off they go, whereas kids who were not in the program have more trouble and need a lot of direction.

Getting Parents/Administrators on Board

You have to get parents and administrators involved if you want their support. One of the things we do at the end of each quarter is to have our students lead conferences with their parents. The first conference, we invite the parents in; second quarter they do it at home because it's around the holidays; for the third quarter we offer an option—traditional teacher/parent conference or a conference between parent and student; and then fourth quarter we have a big culminating project to which we invite the parents.

The most powerful thing about student-led conferences is that kids are responsible for sharing their portfolios and daily binders—the portfolios are best works portfolios and the binders show what the students have done daily—and the kids have to explain what is happening in my classroom. The students have to schedule the appointments and send invitations—some kids prefer to have the conference with another teacher, a coach, or a guidance person (not all parents can be there). We hear a lot from the parents: "OK, we finally understand this." So, one of the ways we get support is to do a lot of inviting—please come into my classroom, please feel free—it gets exhausting, but the benefits are worth it. We also invite other teachers and the administration and guidance in when students have exhibitions.

Planning Time

Any time teachers are going to work together, it's important to have planning time and to meet in places where others can see you are meeting. We really pushed administration a number of years ago until all of us who taught American Studies at the time had a common planning period. We would get together on Wednesdays, third period, and go down to the back of the cafeteria and have our meeting there. This was fairly deliberate and it was worthwhile. If you meet in a place where people can see you are actually using this time—that the schedule hassle is worth it—you will get support. You need to invite people in.

Students Who Like the Old Role

Students who have been very successful at the teacher-directed model of instruction can be fairly uncomfortable with these new approaches. In negotiating comfort level in the classroom, as we make class rules, we try to allow for some kind of a balance. If there are kids who say flat out: "I'm not comfortable with this," or, "The teacher should decide what to do in this case," we'll just work that through with them. I wish I had the magic answer. Part of the answer philosophically for me is that students get lots of time to be in traditional roles. Maybe it's time for others to be comfortable and for you not to be. I don't say that flat out, but I think it.

Breathing Deeply and Diving In

When people ask me how to get started in making the shift from a teacher-centered, top-down classroom situation to a situation where emphasis is on student learning, I often refer them to Nancie Atwell's book In the Middle (1987). Somewhere in there she makes a statement something to the effect that if you are not sure how to begin, just take a deep breath and begin. Start somewhere and try something—try a project where you turn the responsibility over to the students. Yes, everyone has mandated curriculum and we are the specialists. We're supposed to know what is important, but often we don't give the kids enough credit for what they already know or credit for their ability to ask good questions.

I encourage people to use the KNH technique to get started—what do you Know, what do you really Need to know (if you ask them what they want to know, they will often say, " I don't want to know anything."), and How can you learn, How can you get the answers to the question you have? We use this with brainstorming. Or try Barbara Brodhagen's questioning method: "What are your questions about your world; what questions do you have about yourself?" Have students generate a whole list of questions and develop themes from the questions. You will find that that question list is heavily connected to your required curriculum list.

Making the Mind Shift

This is the most difficult part. When kids come and say, "I don't have the research done," or, "I don't have the book," it is so easy to fall into the trap of "Well let me write you a pass," or even, "That's tough, you can't go to your locker." Another way to respond is: "Well, that's a problem. How can you solve it?" Put it right back on them. A young lady said to me a couple of weeks ago, "Well, my partner isn't here so I can't do anything," and I said, "Well, what do you mean—you have the capability to work on these problems yourself—on your proposal." She replied, "Well, I think that's stupid." I said, "I'm sorry you feel that way; however, if you don't work on this, what else could you be doing?"

Practicing What You Will Say

Start by thinking, "What am I going to say when the student says, 'I don't want to?' " Don't get into a power struggle. This isn't a power issue. The students have to be empowered. They are the ones who will or will not learn. "Gee, that's a problem, how do you intend to solve it?" Practice this speech. It's hard to let go. It's particularly hard if you have a flop early on. One of the advantages of being on a team is that you know it's not only you. Somebody is there to support you when things don't go well, and there's someone to celebrate with you when they do go well. The hardest thing for me to deal with was a colleague who said I was abdicating my responsibility as a teacher—that I was being irresponsible in allowing the kids to have so much say in the classroom. That was the toughest confrontation I've ever had, and we're still at an impasse. It is a common misconception that if you have students developing curriculum, students do whatever they want. Constructivist approaches do not mean that. Because students have a choice in a writer's workshop doesn't mean there is no rigor, that the students are doing inappropriate things. This is the real hard one. I have prepared answers for these kinds of questions and at this point I ask if they want to see the contracts my students and I have. Invite people in—let them see what is going on.

Demonstrating

Sometimes you need to do what we call a little "creative insubordination" to do something risky. In other words, just close the door and try it. If it works, share it. Show it to everyone. You have to have confidence in yourself to want to try, but you don't have to make it public up front. Success breeds success. The more others see that what is happening is quite extraordinary in terms of student learning, the more they will support you and will want to try it themselves.

Successes

Not everything has worked the way we wish it would have, but I'll stand by what I wrote a few years ago. That is:

> *Once we began negotiating curriculum with our students, we noticed the conspicuous absence of stereotypical classroom habits. . . . Through the hardships of creating our classes, we experienced democracy in all its complexity. . . . Through negotiating curriculum, the students came to accept more responsibility for their learning. For Ralph and me [and now Rob], the process has affirmed the validity of our basic beliefs about our students. The students have shown us that they really can solve problems—if we just let them. (Smith, 1993, p. 37)*

Special Issues Connected
to Constructivist Approaches

It is almost time for you (whether you are a member of a team or a teacher working alone in a self-contained classroom) to Dive In with projects similar to what teachers describe in this chapter or to at least Get Your Feet Wet with the models and processes in Chapter 6. Before you do, there are two more stops you ought to make on this journey. It would be omitting a major chunk of what is happening in classrooms today if we neglected to talk about technology in relation to constructivist approaches. This we do in the next chapter. It would be even more remiss to try to implement constructivist models without discussing the implications of diversity in our classrooms. Chapter 9, "Making the Most of the Classroom Mosaic," raises important issues about, and provides recommendations for dealing with, diversity.

Tough Questions

1. How will you respond to the parents of your 3rd-grade students when they complain to you that "Elissa, Joel, Rana . . . already studied Native Americans in the 1st and 2nd grade. Why are they doing it again?"

2. When a volunteer parent comes to your 1st-grade classroom and is concerned that the students and not you are leading Calendar Time, what will you do?

3. What will you do when a parent of one of your 4th-grade students goes to the principal to demand that students in your class learn the multiplication tables the way she/he did rather than learning math through problem generating and solving?

4. How would you as a teacher respond to a parent who says, "The middle school is not getting the students ready for high school"?

5. How would you support the statement: "It's more important for students to know how to investigate, create, and problem solve than it is to memorize lots of information."

6. How do you respond to a parent who comes to you with a statement like the following? "My daughter has learned to think and that is good, but sometimes it makes her ask questions she shouldn't—like, 'Why should I have to study this?'"

7. How can you create a learning vision for a middle school team?

8. How can you as a middle school teacher build a bridge from your daily learning goals to the vision?

9. If you try to create a more constructivist classroom in your high school, how will you know if you are preparing the students for college?

10. How could you convince teachers at your high school that students would not be hurt by learning in a different way and perhaps not *covering* as much content, but knowing and understanding more of what they did learn?

11. How can high school teachers work with college professors to reduce the need high school teachers feel to *cover* material?

12. In group project work, how can you weave together the discoveries from each group to make a complete knowledge mosaic for the whole class?

13. In an open process such as student-developed or negotiated curriculum as described in this chapter, what procedures could you develop to keep track of who is doing what?

14. A new teacher, Phil Stevens, tried working with a student-developed curriculum. On the positive side, he found that students were actively involved and interested, they had grasped major issues, and they had learned an area of interest in depth. However, he also found that the following were problems: keeping track of who was doing what and when, finding materials, students turning in poor quality work, and students not having respect for each other's work. If you wanted to try a student-developed curriculum, how would you avoid these problems?

15. Another new teacher, Jeannie Nicholas, who also tried to implement a student-developed curriculum model, found that initially the students were excited. Unfortunately, this was short-lived. As soon as the work became challenging—that is, the students had to brainstorm activities to answer the world and self questions—the group lost enthusiasm and actually didn't do any work for several days. Why might this happen? What would you have done at this point? How could this be avoided?

16. Sean and Yurij, middle school teachers in a rural midwestern area, introduced a student-developed curriculum process to their 5th-grade students. After the students had made lists of questions they had about themselves and their world, they decided their theme for investigations would be "Families." This was a combined social studies and language arts interdisciplinary exploration. Although Sean and Yurij were amazed by the results and how much the students learned about themselves and others, some parents severely disapproved of the project. One parent even threatened to take Sean and Yurij before the superintendent if they continued with the project. What do you think happened here, given this brief scenario? What would you do to avoid this happening in your classroom?

Eight

Untangling the Web

Technology in the Constructivist Classroom

With Peter Weinstein and Jon Margerum-Leys
University of Michigan

This stop on your journey is still under construction and seems to change its character almost every day. Although the amount and kind of technology schools have differ widely, during the 1996-1997 academic year many schools were in a mad rush to get wired; that is, to get networked in the computer lab, networked throughout the school, and networked to cyberspace. A report (1995) from the U.S. Office of Technology Assessment (OTA) estimated that there had been an increase of about 700,000 computers in schools for each of the last 3 years, that about 35% of schools had some kind of computer network, and that almost all schools had TVs and VCRs (O'Neil, 1995). You may be feeling overwhelmed and pressured trying to figure out what this all means, how it all works, and what to do with it all. Have you also asked yourself, How does (or can) any of this enhance learning, and why should I use any of it? How is any of it connected to a constructivist learning experience?

Where Are We Going With Technology in Constructivist Classrooms?

In 1913, Thomas Edison optimistically predicted that books would soon be obsolete, that it would be possible to teach every branch of human knowledge with the motion picture, and that school systems would be completely changed in 10 years (Saettler, 1968). In the 1960s, Skinner believed his teaching machine would revolutionize education; Seymour Papert (1980), developer of LOGO, assured us in the early 1980s that a radical change in education was possible and that change was directly tied to computers— that there would be as much technology in schools as there were pens and pencils. In the late 1980s, Mary Alice White, director of the Electronic Learning Laboratory at Teachers College, Columbia University, contended that technology would alter learning and learning environments, change content, and "enable almost anyone to learn almost anything" (in Levin, 1987, p. 6). We now have the Apple Schools of Tomorrow, all kinds of multimedia systems, and the World Wide Web. According to Clifford Stoll (cited in O'Neil, 1996), however, schools buy and promote technology (usually translated as "computers") with little thought about the educational process. Can technology enhance student learning? Have the schools been duped by media hype and high-powered salespeople?

If you use technology to do the same things you were doing in a traditional format, we would have to ask: Why bother? If, on the other hand, technology can help to develop or to complement and extend constructivist ideas and approaches, then it can be very valuable. The same propositions we have used to define constructivist classrooms thus far are the same propositions you need to use when determining if your use of technology advances or hinders constructivist goals. Are students discovering for themselves? Are they developing problems and questions and then investigating and searching for data? Are they interpreting and synthesizing materials that they find? Are they using the technology to become independent and empowered thinkers who do not depend on the opinions of others? Are students developing new knowledge or simply shuffling information around?

Wired to the Eyeballs: Chatham Lake School

The following story is fictional but is based on classrooms we've visited. All the technology mentioned in this section is currently available and priced within reach of the average school district. As you read this story, ask yourself whether, and in what ways, Chatham Lake is providing constructivist learning approaches for its students.

Chatham Lake School is housed in a single-story red brick building on the outskirts of suburban Detroit. The school services 300 7th- and 8th-grade students with 12 teachers, a full-time principal, and an assistant principal who teaches half-time. Parents come from a variety of backgrounds; many are employed by the nearby auto plant, some work in supporting service industries, and others commute into Detroit. A few families still farm, as evidenced by the occasional bewildered-looking sheep wandering the halls as part of a science project. The cafeteria serves tomato soup and grilled cheese sandwiches every Wednesday.

Differences Between Chatham Lake and Other Schools

Although Chatham Lake School is like hundreds of schools across the United States, there are at least three key differences between Chatham Lake School and the average school. First, Chatham Lake School is wired to the eyeballs. Two years ago, voters passed a bond issue that paid for four computers in each classroom, along with two 30-station labs, a television production studio, and a 15-station mini-lab adjacent to the school media center/library. All computers in the building are hooked into a sophisticated Ethernet-based intranet. This network contains software for creating student projects, classroom and school management software, and shared space for collaboration among students and staff. Students can access their own work from anywhere in the school; all computers are equal on the net. Additionally, all computers in the building are hooked into the Internet. Sophia, the school's full-time tech support staff member, has made sure that the local public library is connected to the school network by a dial-up link, and she has quarterly meetings with the librarians to help them stay up to speed on happenings at Chatham Lake School. With a password and by using the Web to access the link, students and parents can dial into the school network from home at any time of the day or night.

Second, all the staff members at Chatham Lake School teach. Everyone. The principal, Marc, substitutes 1 day a week and has counseling duties. The custodian and the cafeteria staff pitch in for science experiments and vocational awareness projects. Sophia is a full-time computer person, but she rarely spends full days in the network control center. Instead, she is a curriculum specialist who helps teachers and students create meaningful activities that infuse technology as a means rather than an end. In an unusual arrangement, a parent who is certified in elementary education but not currently employed works as the building-level substitute. The results are that classes are kept small, students work with a full range of instructional styles, outside substitutes rarely are needed, and everyone in the building is immediately in touch with classroom issues.

The thing that really sets Chatham Lake School apart, though, is that the teachers realized a few years ago that as nice as things seemed on the surface, the school wasn't really working for kids. After 5 years in the system, students were good at achieving the veneer of success. They could listen diligently to a teacher passing along wisdom, then repeat the wisdom verbatim on multiple-choice and short-answer tests. A chance meeting between a former 6th grader and the principal was the start of an uneasy feeling that this did not constitute learning.

The former student, Jennie, was by this time a high school sophomore. When she met the principal at the grocery store, she just had to tell him all about her high school biology class. She was learning so many new things—all about the water cycle, conservation, and the digestive system of a frog. It was fascinating! Unfortunately, thought the principal, it also was almost exactly the same thing as Jennie supposedly had learned in the 7th grade. She had no idea that she had ever seen the material before, much less mastered it 3 years previously.

When the principal asked other teachers to look carefully at their classrooms and their teaching, it turned out that Jennie's scenario represented a major schoolwide problem. Although students could regurgitate facts for a short while, they were unable to apply what they had learned to real-world situations, could not transfer their knowledge to other subjects, and did not even retain the lists of facts they had learned for any appreciable amount of time.

After reviewing related literature and trying alternative methods of teaching, the teachers came to an unstartling conclusion: For their students to come to clear understandings, they needed to create meaning for themselves. John Dewey had noticed the same thing nearly 100 years previously. Others had noticed this long before that.

As you probably have figured out, some of the teachers in Susan Jackson's school hadn't quite made that leap.

It was clear that teachers were delivering information that had no personal meaning to students. In the name of "covering the material," teachers were rattling through reams of content information; students would rattle it right back and the show would go on.

Marc, the principal, proposed that teachers let go of the delivery model of education, concentrating instead on depth of understanding and authentic learning situations. There was resistance to this: "If we're not teaching the water cycle, are we teaching science at all?" "What if students leave the 6th grade and never hear about Marie Curie?" Marc reminded teachers that students weren't really learning about the water cycle and Marie Curie anyway, so they didn't have much to lose by trying something different.

Today, education differs significantly at Chatham Lake School. Technology enables teachers and students to manage and participate in a different kind of schooling. In the following sections, we provide some snapshots of Chatham Lake School and what schooling in your own district could look like in the future.

Mentoring

Emma is a 6th-grade student at Chatham Lake School. When she first came to the school, she and her parents met with Traci Schimmel, a language arts teacher chosen to be Emma's mentor, to set up short- and long-term goals in an individualized education plan (IEP) for Emma. The format for this plan was borrowed (stolen, really) from special education, which realized long before mainstream education that each student has a unique set of abilities and a unique set of needs. It is the teacher's responsibility to provide rich learning environments and to guide each student through his/her plan. Teachers mentor each one of a group of students on a weekly basis to check on progress with the IEP. The student and teacher make changes together as needed.

Attendance

Emma has the freedom to determine the hours she spends at school. The system ensures that she handles this responsibility in a mature way. Her expected time of arrival is part of her IEP set by Emma, her parents, and her mentor. On a typical morning, Emma arrives between 7 a.m. and 9 a.m. If Emma is needed at home in the morning, she can come in later and either work into the afternoon or work longer on another day. Attendance is automated: Emma punches in by swiping her ID through a card reader at the front door each day. If Emma has not arrived an hour from the time set in her IEP and her absence has not been excused by a phone call, the attendance system automatically calls Emma's parents at work to inform them of her absence. During this phone call, the attendance system gives Emma's parents the opportunity to excuse her absence.

This same attendance system also flags Emma's mentor for follow-up if Emma varies from her IEP time agreement. School administrators have found that unaccounted-for absences have dropped to almost zero, greatly increasing state average daily attendance funding. The flexible attendance policy is important for practical as well as philosophical reasons. Chatham Lake School needs enough equipment to service the school at the busiest time of day. Because the school is open from 7 a.m. to 7 p.m., at any one time half the school might be absent. This means that the computer load is spread throughout the day, greatly reducing the number of workstations needed.

Intranet Journals

Emma's first activity of the day is to work in her on-line journal. Her journal is kept in her on-line folder, which in turn is located on a central server on the school's intranet. Emma's journal has four access levels: public, work group, mentor, and private. Emma's IEP, based on her needs and on state and school curriculum requirements, became the first entry in the private section of Emma's on-line journal. The public level of the journal is used to make announcements, look for working partners, and ask for feedback on works in progress. Many groups choose to publish their work in the public section of the intranet journal.

To be published, projects have to meet certain standards. For example, every project should explicitly define its objectives. Most projects do this by stating a driving question. If the project has clear objectives, it is much easier to judge what a project can and does accomplish. Publishing works on the intranet has two major benefits for the students. First, students have a large audience who can view, comment on, and refer to this work in their own projects. This is extremely motivating. Second, being able to browse other students' work allows students to identify possibilities for projects of their own. The intranet becomes a resource center for teachers and students.

Public Journal Entries

The following is one of Emma's *public journal entries:*

WATER

Authors: *Emma Den Boer, Kevin Wolfram, Marc Andreeson, Yohan Lee*

Project adviser: *Traci Schimmel*

Driving question: *How can we determine if the drinking water in our water fountains is safe to drink?*

How is fountain water different from water in sinks or in toilets? You'll be surprised by the answer! Click here to see our report.

SMOKE RINGS

Did you know that dolphins can blow "smoke rings" made of bubbles? Or that you can make smoke rings of milk in your milk glass at breakfast? Come see us blow smoke rings with a garbage can, flame rings with an acoustic cannon, and talk about the vortex currents which make the rings possible. There's only room for 200, so come early: 3:00 Monday, February 12.

Work Group Journal Entries

Journal entries at the work group level are available to groups of students working on common projects. Some of the journal work groups are social in nature; one of the most active is the work group area on Web publishing. Another popular work group is studying skateboarding. Each student can create and belong to multiple work groups. A basic understanding of all work groups is that any faculty member may read them, but they are not a graded experience.

As with all journal levels, students and faculty can access these on the intranet from any computer at home or in school.

The Volcano project group has just started. A priority for this team will be to define a driving question to focus the inquiry. Right now, the team is gathering background information. From this group, we see the following *work group intranet entry:*

Work Group Volcano Project (sorted by date)

Project adviser: Jamal Cameron

Members: Cherish LaSalle, Emma Den Boer, Julio Alvarez, Scott Parrish

Friday, February 7:

Emma: The stuff I've found so far is in a file called "Volcano Information" in our folder on the 8th grade server. It seems that time of day doesn't matter, based on a database on volcanoes I found on the Web.

Cherish: Time of day for what? Us to look at the information?

Emma: No! Time of day doesn't seem to have anything to do with when volcanoes go off—it could be any time.

Emma: I also found a great archive of pictures. It's at http://www.windows.umich.edu/earth/earth_il.html

Monday, February 10:

Emma: I did some searching on the World Wide Web for information about volcanoes. There's a really good site at http://volcano.und.nodak.edu/vw.html. (Click on the URL to go there)

Mentor Journal Entries

Mentor-level journal entries are available only to school administration, the student, and his or her mentor. These entries are used to monitor progress and give feedback to students. Emma's mentor, Traci Schimmel, finds this area of the journal to be one of the most useful parts of the whole journal. Through it, she is able to give individual attention and feedback to each student she mentors, working at her own pace when she finds time. In the space of half an hour, Traci can interact with half a dozen students, giving her full attention to their needs in a way that would be very difficult in a classroom setting. Take a look at Emma's *mentor journal entry*:

Emma: Where could I go to find information on Morgan horses? I saw a picture of one over the weekend.

Mrs. Schimmel: There are three places you might check: The state of Vermont has a long tradition of raising Morgans. Look at Web pages from the state tourism board. You could also look in the library. We may have some materials. Third, you could ask Paul Mitchell to give you a hand. His group is doing some work on horses.

Mrs. Schimmel: I noticed that last week, you were in for only 3 hours on Friday. Are you okay? Do you have plans to make up the time?

Emma: My dog was sick on Friday and we had to take her to the vet. As it turns out, I was able to get some information for our health project from the vet's office. Can I count that time as school time?

Mrs. Schimmel: If you can get a statement from the vet telling what you talked about and how much time you spent, that might be okay.

Private Journal Entries

Emma also has a private level of her journal, for thoughts still in the formative stage or for thoughts she would rather not share. Emma's standard practice is to work on all new material first in the private section of her journal, moving it to more public spaces as she becomes more comfortable with the writing and content.

After looking over the public section of her intranet journal, Emma reviews the work groups sections of her journal. She's been frustrated with her volcanoes work group: Some of the other members of the group aren't pulling their weight. Since her last set of postings to the work group on Monday, no action has taken place. Emma notes her frustration in the personal section of her journal, making a mental note to bring the issue up with the group's project adviser. Here is a sample of her *private journal entry*:

I'm getting sick of doing all the work in our group on volcanoes. How can I tell Mrs. Schimmel about the problem without seeming like a tattletale?

Paul is soooooooooooooooooooooooooooooooooo cute! I want his school picture for my locker!!!!!!!!!!!!!!!!!!!!!!!!!!!!!!!!!!!!!

Rusted Root ROCKS

Reminder: Get a note from the vet saying that we talked about health project.

Reminder: Get mom to stop packing yogurt in my lunch. I found out today in our bio group that yogurt has living things in it. GROSS

After checking in with her journal, Emma spends an hour or so getting ready for her volcano project work group meeting. Most of that time, Emma is at a computer in the media center. From there, she is able to gather data from the World Wide Web, which she posts in the work group section of her journal. Today, however, Emma is meeting with her volcano work group. One of its members, Cherish, went to Hawaii over winter break. She came back with some great photos of active volcanoes and a desire to learn more about volcanoes. After putting the photos into the public intranet space and asking for help, Cherish was joined by Emma, Julio, and Scott. They found a teacher, Jamal Cameron, who was willing to act as the adviser for this project. The five of them sat down with their IEPs to set goals for the project. They used the PIViT program (Project Integration Visualization Tool) to set goals for projects and develop questions to be answered.

PIViT

Students at Chatham Lake School use the PIViT (Project Integration Visualization Tool) software to map out their projects. PIViT allows students to create a complex project map, linking questions, concepts, curricular objectives, investigations, classroom activities, and assessment items/artifacts—the same kind of process students should be using to develop a nontechnology project. Additionally, they can link the project plan to a calendar built into PIViT. Their project plan can be color coded to indicate which students are responsible for which tasks.

Emma, Scott, Julio, and Cherish have set up their project on volcanoes so that Emma is responsible for the question "What conditions are necessary for a volcano to erupt?" Scott is working on "Geographically, where do these conditions exist?" Cherish is trying to determine if volcano eruptions can be predicted, and Julio is concentrating on past, present, and possible future volcanic activity in Michigan. They entered these questions and related subquestion/topics into the PIViT program and now have a color-coded project map that links together all the information and provides a clear illustration, for both teachers and other students, of the focus and intended work.

Workgroup Meetings

The students at today's meeting of the volcano group gather at a table in the library. On a whiteboard at the front of the room, Jamal writes some categories for discussion:

Questions researched
New questions uncovered
Progress?

Each student writes with a different colored marker, and the categories fill up. Everything written on the whiteboard is automatically transferred to a file on the attached personal computer; this file will serve as a record of the meeting, and each student's mentor teacher will view this record as a part of ongoing assessment. Additionally, students who are unable to attend a meeting can stay abreast of meeting progress—either while the meeting is happening or after the meeting has finished—by getting on line.

Math Class at Chatham

Emma never used to like math all that much. She couldn't figure out why it was important to do things like memorize her multiplication tables or work out math facts. The math classes at Chatham Lake School are different: Each class lasts 6 weeks and addresses a specific math topic. Class offerings are scheduled around the needs of work groups. At the initial session of a work group, the members and their project adviser determine which math skills will be helpful to and necessary for them in their project. These are submitted to the math department, which schedules the classes. Often, the math needs of several work groups will converge, allowing for a full classroom of 24-30 students. For Emma's group and the work of three other work groups, the math department is offering a course on measurement and conversion. Today, they'll look at converting centigrade and Kelvin temperature readings to Fahrenheit.

You, Your School, and Technology

You probably don't work at Chatham. What is important is that you have seen how technology can change a whole system of schooling and learning. What is happening at your school with technology? Has the school just purchased and networked computers? Are you wondering how to use them? What technology do you have available to you? How, how often, when, and why do you use the technology in your school?

Avoiding the Filmstrip Trap

Have you ever watched what happens when a teacher tells a class they are going to view a videotape, a filmstrip, or a TV show? Usually, the students tune out, catch up on lost sleep, or, if they are teenagers, pass notes around about the Saturday night party. Regardless of the time spent in preparation for the presentation or use of these technologies, unless the teacher has found an extraordinary prepackaged program, which most are not, he or she will lose the students. If you've ever used these programs yourself, you know that even you might be napping, correcting papers, or daydreaming.

What do you see when students are using computers? What we have seen and see often are students typing reports that consist merely of words taken from the Web or students spending a whole class period trying to draw the funniest nose for a science report about smell or a student dragging clip art around and making "click here" buttons so other students can look at various pieces of this art, which the students then connect to a few sentences and call a report. This is not active learning. Clearly, just using lots of technology does not guarantee that you are using constructivist approaches. Students need to be actively involved in their own learning. As long as they are passive, as with the "sit and watch" or with the "sit, input, watch, move objects and text around, then sit, input, and move objects and text around some more" use of educational media, they will suffer terminal (sorry, no pun intended) boredom. As Rousseau might say, they will become stupid and passive. In any event, they will learn little.

What Is Technology Anyway?

A common mistaken idea is that computers represent the only educational technology available. This is not so. If you are in a school that has few computers, you don't have to panic. There are many kinds of technology you can use to complement and create constructivist classrooms. Let's look at some of the technology you probably already use or have used and see how you might use it to advance constructivist goals.

The Overhead Projector

If you use the overhead projector to show notes or diagrams to the students, that is a traditional format. As helpful and as necessary as this may be in your classes at various times and for various purposes, there are other ways to use the overhead. For example, in any of the models referred to in Chapter 5, once students have decided on an investigation or activity, they need to find, interpret, and synthesize their material and demonstrate understanding. Students can show that they have analyzed and that they understand material or have solved problems by using overheads and a tape recorder. They can create the overheads by drawing visuals such as diagrams, charts, or figures that would clearly indicate analysis and comprehension of the topic; they can then write a complementary script and record this on an audiotape that will accompany the overhead visuals. This tape can either introduce provocative questions relating to the drawings or create related problems for the whole class to solve. A group of 5th graders from an inner-city Indianapolis school that had almost no technology equipment (and a very, very old overhead projector) created a similar demonstration for their project in National History Day a few years ago and blew the judges (professional historians) away with their in-depth analysis. The point is that you don't need complicated technology to allow students to create, demonstrate, and enhance investigation and learning.

Slides and Slide Shows

Slides have a major advantage as an instructional medium over other media for two reasons. First, they are easy to produce by both teachers and students. Because it is the students or teacher who produce the slides, the slides have more meaning, relevance, and authenticity for the students than do professionally developed slides (Heinich, Molenda, Russell, & Smaldino, 1996). Second, the crisp image resolution is far superior to anything a typical school computer can generate. This clear image leads to a completely different response and experience on the part of the student audience. We know, however, that slide shows can be boring, and if a show is nothing but a travelogue or another version of a teacher telling something to somebody—except with pictures—then it's just another spin on traditional formats. The slides and the slide show are not the end—they are, as with overheads, the means through which students demonstrate that they have analyzed and understood an issue or problem, or they are the means through which students can present new problems for the class to solve. As part of the process of investigating and figuring out, students can create a script to accompany the slides.

They can add appropriate music that adds to the demonstration of understanding or enhances the issues for other students. Finally, they can engage class members by asking them to analyze slides in various ways.

This can be as simple as a student manually running a slide projector while discussing the issues or as complicated as one or more students preparing an audiotape of their narration, then pulsing the tape to drive the slide show. The latter requires some specialized equipment such as a dissolve unit, a sound mixer, and a unit with which to lay pulses on the master audiotape. You can read more about this in a book called *Slide Showmanship* by Elinor Stecker (1987) or in the book *Instructional Media and Technologies for Learning* (Heinich et al., 1996). What goes into creating the slide show—doing library research, interviewing by phone or in person famous and not-so-famous people, reviewing primary sources, taking live and book photos, analyzing the material, writing a script, and merging it all into an understandable and provocative production—is what makes this exercise constructivist. National History Day at the University of Maryland also can provide examples of these shows for you.

Documentary Video Making

Many students now have video cameras, and many schools have at least one camera that students can use. Some schools have editing equipment, and others have the local cable station housed in their building. Cable stations allow students to do more sophisticated technical work and often allow them to broadcast their video throughout the school network. Although students have to learn how to use the camera and the editing equipment, it is once again the research and investigation, the interviewing, the analysis, and the synthesis into a final product that is constructivist.

If students fall asleep when watching filmstrips and videos and TV programs, why won't they fall asleep when student productions are used? There is research (Page, 1992) to indicate that the opposite occurs when students develop the media productions. Students in the audience become actively involved and curious about these peer productions and messages. Remember Marshall McLuhan's (1967) *The Medium Is the Massage*? When student productions are the medium, it makes a difference for the audience. Why would this be?

Here is what some student participants in National History Day thought about this issue:

> Jim thought students were actively engaged when watching other students' media productions because the students wanted to evaluate their own presentation in relation to some other student's. Ed and Amosh, however, argued that it had more to do with knowing how difficult developing a media presentation was and in having empathy for the student producer. Amosh also argued that adolescents were more trusting of other adolescents and would put more stock in a student's presentation than in a professionally developed one because "they're [the professionals] paid to do that and you kind of get this negative thing in your mind." (Page, 1992, p. 328)

Computers

The story of Chatham Lake School provides the ultimate in how computers and technology can alter the entire organizational system of schooling as well as the nature of the learning experience. We recognize, however, that many schools still have few computers and many schools are just in the process of setting up computer labs. For those of you working in these schools, we have included in this section some ways that you can use computers in existing traditional school systems and still have constructivist learning experiences.

Computers and Software

We'll start with the simplest use of computers. Some software currently on the market can facilitate constructivist learning experiences; other software is dreadful and does nothing but reinforce traditional methods or drill and repeat. Most educational programs developed for sale in retail stores are what we call *edutainment*. They are loaded with razzle dazzle that is simply irrelevant to the task. Sometimes the real task, if you look closely, is not what is advertised as educational but something else that is quite trivial. For example, a well-known program that claims to teach geography does not in fact demand any use of geography to complete the sequence of activities. The student is required only to do some rudimentary pattern matching of pictures. Although the student may pick up some geographical trivia, she is not likely to develop any deep under-standing of the subject by playing the game.

True constructivist programs engage students in extended prob-lem solving. The best software packages we have found belong to Tom Snyder Productions of Watertown, Massachusetts. Everything that company produces is focused on and grounded in constructivist propositions.

Table 8.1 provides a short list of criteria that can be used to iden-tify the essential philosophy of an educational software program. Some programs may have characteristics of more than one type, and some programs don't fit any category well.

Computers and Multimedia Systems

Some schools have multimedia computer systems that allow stu-dents to combine many technologies and materials in one place. This is true of an Apple School of Tomorrow school where some of our student teachers work. This technology can include a digital camera with which students can take pictures that are then fed right into the computer program or learning experience that the students are de-veloping. It can include a video camera that is connected to the com-puter and allows students to feed video into the planned document, along with the still pictures. Additionally, scanners can scan into the same document any pictures or words the students have or that they create. To add to this, students can retrieve materials from the Web, from libraries, and from e-mail lists. There is also sound capability connected to these setups. If students use all this equipment to sim-ply retrieve, input, and move information or visuals around, this is not constructivist. You want true investigating, figuring out, and problem solving to occur. The final document should be the result of the student's analysis, interpretation, and synthesis of all gathered or produced material.

What Do Chatham Lake and Your School Have in Common?

At Chatham Lake, constructivist software and powerful integrated networks and hardware are making it possible for the student to be in the driver's seat. Emma is developing deep understandings be-

TABLE 8.1 Identifying the Philosophy of a Software Program

Criteria for Classifying Software	Information Delivery (transmission)	Edutainment	Constructivist
Way student spends time	Student is active, but mostly absorbing rather than using information	Student spends a lot of time passively watching the screen	Student is active, engaged in problem solving. Software can be used to create permanent products
Who controls the sequence of activity	The computer	Usually the computer	The student
Way of confirming and acknowledging learning	The student passes tests or quizzes and is usually rewarded with audiovisual congratulations	The student completes the sequence and is reward with audiovisual congratulations	The student produces a product that may be shown to and evaluated by other students, teachers, or members of the community
Mental state after extended use	Student often becomes tired	Eyes glaze over	Student remains alert and engaged

cause it is her voice that comes through in the group projects and her voice that is heard in her journal and on the intranet. For faculty and staff at Chatham Lake, having appropriate technology at their fingertips means being able to hear students' voices and to manage the messiness that is a part of any constructivist learning environment.

Your school probably has similar goals connected to student learning and experiences. If so, you can address these goals using the technology you have. It is important not to discard what you have known or have now as technology but to work at using these older and different technologies and the newer technologies for the same purpose—to make learning experiences active and student owned.

There Is No End to This Chapter

One chapter in a book that focuses on how to create constructivist classrooms cannot do justice to the issues, advances, possibilities, and questions connected to technology. Additionally, there is so much happening so quickly with regard to technology in schools that much of this chapter probably is outdated as we write. We also know we have left out important items here. We hope the coauthors of this chapter will write the book needed to finish this chapter. What we have done is provide you with a beginning. It's your turn to make it happen. Get cracking.

Tough Questions

1. How do you as a teacher get over your anxiety connected to using technology?
2. How can teacher education programs in colleges with little technology prepare students to be teachers who will need to know how and when to use technology in constructivist classrooms?
3. How can any school or teacher keep up with the changes that occur in the field of technology?
4. How would you monitor and maintain constructivist approaches in a school like Chatham Lake?
5. What, about Chatham Lake, from the little you know about it, models constructivist propositions?
6. How would you feel about working in Chatham Lake and why?
7. How would you go about demonstrating to fellow teachers the difference between technology use in a constructivist class and technology use in a traditional class?
8. What would you change, or add to what you know, about Chatham Lake to develop more constructivist learning experiences?

Nine

Making the Most of the Classroom Mosaic

Recently, we visited a student teacher in a small elementary school in the northwestern corner of rural Vermont. Imagine our surprise to find a sign on the front door for parents, written in Vietnamese! Schools are changing, and they are changing fast. The arrival of new immigrant groups, the mainstreaming of children with disabilities, and the precipitous rise in poverty among children have all contributed to making our classrooms more diverse—and in more ways—than at any other time in our nation's history. In fact, children are the most diverse segment of American society. Although student diversity makes teaching more challenging, this is problematic only if the focus is on how the teacher will deliver instruction rather than on how the students will learn. Classroom settings with students from different cultures, abilities, needs, and interests provide rich learning opportunities, in part because they so clearly reflect one of the central tenets of constructivism: There is virtually an infinite variety of ways to know the world. The magnitude of student diversity underscores this point in ways impossible to ignore by even the most traditional of teachers.

How Are Our Schools Changing?

Consider the following.

- Close to 60% of the nation's entire immigrant population entered the United States in the 1980s. A century ago, the nations that sent the largest numbers of immigrants had a common European culture (England, Ireland, Germany, and Italy). The nations that send the most immigrants now—and that are projected to do so through at least the year 2000—come from every corner of the globe. In rank order, they are Mexico, the Philippines, Korea, China, Taiwan, India, Cuba, the Dominican Republic, Jamaica, Canada, Vietnam, the United Kingdom, and Iran (Hodgkinson, 1993).

- As a group, children are America's poorest citizens. During the 1980s, the poverty rate for children reached an unprecedented 11%; by 1993, the level had increased to 23% (or more than 1 in 5 school-aged children; Hodgkinson, 1993).

- The two largest minority groups are African Americans (30 million) and Hispanic Americans (20 million). Together, they will compose about one third of the total school enrollment by the year 2000; currently, non-European American students are the majority in the 25 largest school districts in the country (Hodgkinson, 1992).

- More than 15% of students in the schools of New York, Chicago, Los Angeles, Washington, D.C., and San Francisco are of limited English proficiency (Hodgkinson, 1992).

- The United States Bureau of the Census estimates that there are 329 languages other than English spoken in the United States (Sileo, Sileo, & Prater, 1996).

Do These Differences Affect Learning?

Simply put, "Yes." There is overwhelming evidence that such factors as a student's country of origin, cultural heritage, linguistic background, and religious beliefs, as well as the socioeconomic status of the student's parents, all, in their own way, influence learning. Teachers who fail to recognize how the values of traditional schooling may clash with particular cultural values (Kugelmass, 1995) often face classrooms of disengaged, unmotivated, and/or disruptive learners who may find school irrelevant, or even hostile, to their values.

The Problem

As suggested above, today's teachers are required to be sensitive to a wider range of multicultural differences than ever before. Most teachers in the United States are white. By century's end, more than one third of the school-aged population will be nonwhite; "minority" students already are the majority culture in many large urban school districts. Although eager to learn, teachers as a group believe they are unprepared to teach students from diverse cultures (Barry & Lechner, 1995). Can teachers package content into a single format that all children can understand? Or should they continuously repackage the content for each of the cultural, religious, and ethnic groups represented in their classrooms?

Liberating Ourselves

Framing the issues in this way reveals the potency of teacher commitment to thinking about teaching as information dispensing. As Barry and Lechner (1995) report, teachers are concerned primarily with how they will relate content in multiple ways to meet the needs of a very diverse student body. It should come as no surprise that teachers feel that this is a daunting task for which they are ill prepared. In fact, this is not a daunting task at all; it is an impossible one. Although some find this enormously distressing, we believe it is very liberating; as teachers, we cannot simultaneously be all things to all children. Nor can we present one approach based on a kind of average of student difference. Rather, we must reframe our questions about teaching and learning. We must do so to allow for student exploration and inquiry in a way that allows them to connect content knowledge to what they already know. How is this possible for students with limited English proficiency? How can teachers meet the needs of Mexican American children, children of Asian Pacific descent, and African American children, all of whom are in the same classroom?

Focusing on Students' Experiences

Ethnic differences are real, but continually seeking to alter our teaching style to conform to our beliefs about each student (based

solely on his or her ethnic identity) perpetuates an overgeneraliza-
tion about ethnic groups and puts the focus of the teaching/learning
experience in the wrong place. Knowing that Asian children as a
group are quieter and more submissive to authority will not enhance
the learning of students of Asian descent if, as a teacher armed with
this knowledge, you continue to focus on what you will do to cover
the curriculum as opposed to focusing on the ways you can help
your students connect content to the most important factors in student learning—the students' experiences and prior knowledge
(Ausubel, 1968).

The value of constructivism is that it respects and allows each student to use his or her unique knowledge and experience in the learning process. This is so whether the student is from a 10,000-acre ranch
in Billings, Montana, or a one-room flat in Springfield, Massachusetts.

Classroom Culture and Ethnic Culture: A Dynamic Relationship

Looking at Two Ethnic Groups: Vietnamese and Navajo

Many books that address the teaching of different ethnic groups
describe Vietnamese (and in general Asian) children as being quiet,
submissive, and reluctant to speak publicly, and Navajo children as
being nonverbal, nonanalytical, and even disengaged. Review Table
9.1, but be advised: It is detrimental to the learning health of your
students.

In Traditional Classrooms

The traits described in Table 9.1 appear primarily when the diverse classroom is one where the teacher dispenses knowledge. In
these classrooms, teachers of minority students spend more time
talking than do teachers of white children; thus, minority children
"spend considerably more time listening than being heard" (Moran
in McCarty, Lynch, Wallace, & Benally, 1991, p. 54). When communication is controlled by the teacher, when students are singled out to
answer direct questions about subjects "for which they have little
background knowledge" (Collier, Laatsch, & Ferrero, 1972, p. 70),

TABLE 9.1 Questioning Stereotypes

Ethnicity	Learning Style	Implications for Teaching
Asian	Quiet, submissive, obedient, prefer not to call attention to themselves, prefer to work independently, reluctant to engage in "free discussion," prefer not to partake in brainstorming exercises.	Didactic methods important, teachers should transmit information, strategies, etc. through lecture. Teachers should understand if student does not ask questions, is reluctant to challenge assumptions/methods of teacher, or otherwise appears unengaged.
Navajo	Nonanalytical, nonverbal, visual learners, "doers" rather than "talkers" (McCarty, Lynch, Wallace, & Benally, 1991), may consider it rude to disagree in public, or not worth the risk of hurting someone's feelings by stating an opinion in class, often slow to respond verbally.	Teacher should employ "right hemisphere" approaches, emphasizing dance, art, and music. Teachers should employ a lot of wait time after questions. Try to avoid asking direct questions that put students on the spot.

this very classroom culture reinforces submissiveness and makes certain minority groups appear, as groups, to be nonverbal, nonanalytical, or disengaged.

In Constructivist Classrooms

The situation is different in constructivist classrooms. Where

teachers and students share talk, where the expression of students' ideas is sought and clearly valued, where curricular content meaningfully incorporates the students' social environment, and where students use their cultural and linguistic

resources to solve new problems, Native American students respond eagerly and quite verbally to questioning, even in their second language. (McCarty et al., 1991, p. 53)

According to Steinberg (1996), Asian students outperform all
other groups (including whites) on measures of school performance.
They earn higher grades, do more homework, cut class less often,
and report less mind-wandering. One of Steinberg's most striking
findings, however, is that compared to all other ethnic groups,
Asians so frequently "turn to each other for academic assistance and
consultation" (p. 47). They collaborate, they work in groups, they
pose questions, and they work on them together. This is hardly what
one would expect based on Table 9.1, which characterizes Asians as
independent, passive, and reluctant to ask questions.

In a study by McCarty and colleagues (1991), the use of a pilot
curriculum that emphasized open-ended questioning, collaborative
group work, and student-directed learning (not exactly the approach
suggested in Table 9.1) was shown to enhance student engagement,
content mastery, and analytic reasoning in Navajo youth. As suggested in Table 9.1 above, this approach was widely considered to be
antithetical to the Navajo learning style. As Au pointed out (in
McCarty et al., 1991), "Native American children may in no way be
characterized as nonverbal . . . though . . . there are settings in which
they may appear so" (p. 53). Unfortunately, these settings all too
often are our classrooms.

Two Approaches

Let's turn to a more practical example of these points. Think about
the assumptions that inform and guide the different educational approaches presented below:

Approach 1: Monday-Thursday, a 10th-grade biology teacher presents a 40-minute lecture each afternoon on the digestive system
of sheep, their eating habits, and their grazing preferences. When
a student asks a question about the content during the lectures,
the teacher provides the answer. If the teacher poses a question to
which a student responds incorrectly, the teacher provides the
right answer or turns to another student until she gets the correct

response. She then moves on. On Friday, she gives a multiple-choice test based on the information covered during the week. Her evaluation of a student's learning is based on the student's test score. Although she may never return to the subject of sheep for the remainder of the year, the teacher is confident that a high score indicates that a student has learned the material and that she has adequately "covered" the content.

Approach 2: Monday-Thursday, an elder Navajo sheep herder spends 40 minutes with tribal children each afternoon listening to their questions about sheep, their eating habits, and their grazing preferences. When a child asks a question, the elder replies "What do *you* think?" and continues to encourage further observation and inquiry (McCarty et al., 1991). On Friday, the elder asks the children to herd the sheep without him, to rely on one another, and to return prepared to demonstrate what they have learned. Gradually, children become responsible for the herding of sheep. Their mastery of the content information is continuously tied to, and used as a foundation for, subsequent learning.

Though fictional and time-compressed, these scenarios encapsulate much of what we know about the importance of a constructivist perspective in diverse classroom settings: Children, regardless of their cultural heritage, are curious, active explorers and constructors of their worlds. Navajo children, however, may not appear so inclined in **Approach 1**—in fact, they typically are characterized (as noted in Table 9.1) as passive and disengaged. Yet, as McCarty and colleagues (1991) demonstrated, in educational settings that encourage children to tie new content to their own experience, that are conducive to give-and-take, and that facilitate exploration and experimentation, Navajo children are active learners who pose questions, make hypotheses, and draw conclusions based on their own analyses. Traditional classroom settings may reinforce not only submissiveness in many cultures, but dependence as well. If you believe that children in **Approach 2** know and will remember more about sheep than children in **Approach 1**, this suggests that a reasonable goal would be to set up your classroom in ways that encourage questioning, experimentation, and collaboration (with or without live sheep).

Disabilities and Academic Failure

Individuals With Disabilities Education Act

Since the passage of the Education of All Handicapped Children Act (PL 94-142) in 1975, all children, regardless of disability, have been entitled to a free and appropriate public education. This federal law (amended in 1990 and now referred to as the Individuals With Disabilities Education Act or IDEA) is both a civil rights landmark and a landmark in the history of American education. IDEA prohibits the exclusion of disabled students from public schools (which was routine in some states prior to 1975) and requires that children with disabilities be educated with their nondisabled peers to the maximum extent appropriate (i.e., in the least restrictive environment). IDEA also requires school personnel to

- construct individualized education plans (for students with disabilities);
- closely monitor student progress; and
- evaluate the academic achievement and cognitive ability of identified students on a regular basis.

Despite the progressive nature of special education legislation, individuals with identified disabilities, as a group, continue to fare poorly both in our schools and in their transition to adulthood. Who are the students with disabilities in our schools? Table 9.2 provides some of the answers.

Educational Outcomes for Students With Disabilities

Here is some of what we know:

- Although about 1 in 10 students receives special education services, many more school-aged children are presumed to have disabilities. Nationally, about 65% of students with disabilities receive at least some of their instruction in the context of the regular classroom. In some states (e.g., Colorado and Vermont), more than 80% of students with disabilities spend most, if not all, of their day in a regular classroom (Turnbull, Turnbull, Shank, & Leal, 1995).

TABLE 9.2 Disability Type and Incidence

Disability	Percentage of All Students With Disabilities
Specific learning disabilities: Students of average intellectual ability or higher with significant difficulty in one or more academic domains (e.g., reading)	49.9
Speech or language impairment: Students with significant difficulty in either producing language (e.g., articulation difficulty) or understanding language (e.g., following directions)	22.2
Mental retardation: Students with significantly below-average measured intellectual ability *and* age-appropriate social skills (e.g., communication, independent living, etc.)	12.3
Serious emotional disturbance: Students with chronic emotional, behavioral, or interpersonal difficulties extreme enough to interfere with learning	8.9
Multiple disabilities: Students with more than one disability	2.2
Orthopedic impairments: Students who have limited functional use of legs, feet, arms, hands, or other body parts	1.1
Other health impairments: Students with chronic conditions that limit strength, vitality, or alertness (e.g., epilepsy, arthritis, asthma)	1.3
Hearing impairments: Students with significant hearing loss in one or both ears	1.3
Visual impairments: Students with low vision, even when corrected	0.5

(continued)

TABLE 9.2 Continued

Disability	Percentage of All Students With Disabilities
Deaf-blindness: Students with both significant hearing loss and low vision	< 0.1
Autism: Students with significant difficulty in both social interaction and communication	< 0.1
Traumatic brain injury: Students who have had brain injury as the result of external force (e.g., car accident) or internal occurrence (e.g., stroke)	< .01

SOURCE: Yeseldyke and Algozzine, 1995.

- In 1992, about 3 million children were receiving child protective services for abuse and/or neglect (Turnbull et al., 1995).
- One in 5 school-aged children is estimated to have reading disabilities (Lyon, 1995; Shaywitz, 1995). Eighty percent of students with weak reading skills who fail to make significant reading progress by the age of 9 will continue to be unskilled readers in the 10th grade (Shaywitz, 1995).
- Since 1977, the identification of emotional-behavioral disorders has risen by 32%; in some states, this number has increased by more than 75% (Carnine, 1994). Nationally, the identification of learning disabilities has more than doubled between 1977 and 1994. There are currently well more than 2 million school-aged children identified with learning disabilities (Turnbull et al., 1995).
- Close to 3 million school-aged children take Ritalin every day.
- Nationally, the dropout rate is 25%; only about 50% of students with disabilities graduate from high school. Between 1980 and 1990, the prison population in the United States increased by 139% (Hodgkinson, 1992); recent rate increases are estimated at 300% (Carnine, 1994). Of America's prisoners, 82% are high school dropouts; 75% to 80% of the prison population is esti-

mated to have specific learning disabilities and/or serious emotional disturbance.

- Juel (1988) found that about 40% of unskilled readers in the 4th grade would prefer cleaning their rooms to reading.

Connections to Traditional Classrooms?

Why is the "dropout" rate so high for students with disabilities? Why is academic underachievement so prevalent? Why have behavioral problems increased so dramatically? Why do students prefer cleaning their rooms to reading? The answers to these questions are complex and multifaceted, and they are clearly beyond the scope of this book. We must ask, though, to what extent teaching approaches that focus on the transmission of information contribute to student failure, disengagement, and disenfranchisement. Is it plausible in all (or even most) cases of student failure that students and/or their families are to blame for weak academic skills and/or behavioral problems? Goodlad (1984) found that students spend a little more than 10% of their time in school asking questions, reading, writing, or engaged in some other form of active learning. Is there something wrong with our children, or are schools and teachers contributing to this state of affairs? Could 5,000 reports be right in finding that no student difficulty was related to shortcomings in school practice? Or would Carnine's (1994) question about this finding ring more true: "If 5,000 medical files of patients who failed to respond to [medical] treatment were analyzed, would there be an absence of professional shortcomings in all 5,000 cases?" (Carnine, 1994, p. 341).

Could it be the teaching approach that makes difference in the classroom so deadly? Think about Sam, whom you met in the fable in Chapter 5. Can some of his school difficulties be attributed to shortcomings related to school practice? Or do you think that, like thousands of others with his profile of strengths and weaknesses, Sam needs to either conform to traditional schooling or get out?

The Challenge

Disabilities make learning and classrooms more challenging. Some disabilities may even make the learning of some things impossible. As teachers, we must create opportunities for learning that are more exciting, more enriching, and more rewarding—in short, more appealing—than the desire to clean one's room, leave school, get involved in criminal activity, or become a ward of the state. During the 1980s, in Massachusetts, some urban school systems reported 20% or more of the entire student population in special education programs. Where did all these special education students come from? "Were they sitting undetected in regular classrooms, or have special education mandates provided a fast track out of regular education for problem learners?" (Henley, Ramsey, & Algozzine, 1993, p. 183). Others have noted that a focus on the ways in which students do not fit into traditional classrooms (in addition to putting system and teacher needs ahead of student needs) also often reflects cultural biases. For example:

> Only when formal education came to the Indian Nations were labels supplied to the differences between children. Public Law 94-142 . . . caused multitudes of children to be labeled mentally retarded or learning disabled who up until that time were not considered handicapped in their cultures. (Locust, in Turnbull et al., 1995, p. 15)

The Regular Education Initiative and the Full Inclusion Movement

Full Inclusion Is Changing Classrooms

For the last 20 years, most special education students received a large part of their education in public schools—but on a "pull-out" basis. Most still do. That is, students leave their regular classrooms for part or all of the day to work with a special education teacher or aide in a resource room on individual academic skills or behavioral goals. Most students with disabilities still receive the bulk of their education in resource rooms; however, including students with disabilities in regular classrooms for most or all of their day (regardless of the severity of their disability) has become increasingly popular around the nation. This change in thinking has been variously described as the "full inclusion" or "mainstreaming" movement. Several persuasive arguments have driven this change.

Problems With Pull-Out Programs

First, research on the ineffectiveness of tracking by ability groups demonstrates that, in general, students perform better academically in heterogeneous, rather than homogeneous, groupings (Lewis, 1990). Madeline Will, once the Assistant Secretary for Special Education and Rehabilitative Services, noted, in a frequently cited address (1985), that special education students were dropping out of school at very high rates each year, despite intensive efforts. She argued that special and regular education be merged, because in her view the negative side effects of special education—its high cost, the stigmatization of students, the fragmentation of instruction into self-contained special and regular education units, the student dropout rate—outweighed any benefit it might confer on students with disabilities.

Although research shows (Henley et al., 1993) that special needs students appear to do better in regular classrooms than in special education settings, recent surveys indicate that most teachers are uncomfortable with special education students in their classrooms because they feel that they do not have the proper training to work with students with disabilities. Are these fears justified? Perhaps, but in some sense, this appears irrelevant, as virtually every public school classroom (K-12) has at least one student with a disability; teachers must learn to adjust to mainstreaming, regardless of their politics. Still, legitimate questions remain. Do students with disabilities require something regular education teachers cannot provide? What is it that special education teachers provide that is so critical to the needs of students with disabilities? What additional training do regular education teachers need to ensure that students with disabilities receive an appropriate education in their classrooms?

What's So Special About Special Education?

As it turns out, very little. There is some good news about what works (and what does not) for students with disabilities. What we can say with certainty about what students with disabilities need is contrary to what many regular (and special) educators believe.

False Assumptions

For example, many classroom teachers operate under the assumption that only specialized training in fields like learning disabilities, mental retardation, and speech and language disorders will allow them to work effectively with disabled students in their classrooms. Similarly, many special educators believe that they are somehow uniquely qualified (by virtue of their training) to work with children with disabilities. Many assume that the magic bullet for working with students with disabilities is finding the right placements and particular academic or behavioral curricula that match the disability in question. We now know, from a variety of research, that all these assumptions are false. In fact, Ysseldyke and Algozzine (1995) have summarized these findings by noting that research in special education has been unable to demonstrate that

- specific instructional practices/techniques match or work better with specific learner characteristics; research has not supported the view that children with mental retardation need X, whereas children with learning disabilities need Y;
- certain placements result in improved academic achievement; or
- special educators are more effective in working with students with disabilities than are regular educators.

How Can I Teach Special Education Kids in My Classroom?

As you probably could have guessed by now, this is the wrong question.

Asking the Right Question

How do students learn? How can I spark their curiosity, facilitate their learning, and get out of their way? These questions are ultimately more important, particularly for students with disabilities, who are at increased risk of school failure. The high school dropout rate for students with disabilities continues to be very high. Without a compelling reason to stay, and with little academic success and much frustration, this should come as no surprise. For many students with disabilities, school is deadly boring; it is irrelevant to their lives, needs, and interests; and for many others, it is extremely punishing as well.

What Do Students With Disabilities Need?

The value of special education can be summed up as follows: What's good for the goose is necessary for the gander. That is, although all students benefit from good teachers, students with a history of academic and/or behavioral challenges (for whatever reason) *need* good teachers and the kind of classroom experiences supported by and driven by constructivist propositions, including the proposition that student talent and ability can be key to developing knowledge. If a teacher is simply delivering information, he cannot ever deal with the infinite variety of perspectives (in the case of ethnic questions) or with the different ways of knowing and learning that students with disabilities present. To remain interested and engaged in learning, students need opportunities to discover, create, and problem solve. What if problem solving skill is precisely what they lack?

Building Bridges: Putting Students in Control of Their Learning

Two Approaches

Many teachers treat students with disabilities as if they have a defect that needs correcting. To fix the disability, some professionals believe that students need high levels of teacher-directed information transmission. This approach often relies on prepackaged remedial programs such as the Orton-Gillingham Reading Method and standardized ways to assess learning. At the other extreme, some advocate fostering student strengths (wherever they may be), following the students' lead in learning, and letting students choose whether or not to attempt to improve the academic skill areas in which they may struggle. The first approach often results in the temporary memorization of increased content knowledge. Resource room teachers, for example, often report a threshold effect: When students leave the resource room and cross the door's threshold, everything they learned seems to have vanished. The second approach also is inappropriate for many students with disabilities because most disabilities, including specific learning disabilities and attentional disorders (the majority of the disability pie), are frequently characterized by weak ability to approach tasks in a planful and strategic manner and to carefully monitor ongoing performance (Marlowe, 1990). Thus, the majority of students with disabilities do not spontaneously initiate problem-solving behaviors, and they demonstrate difficulty sustaining attention, inhibiting impulsive responding, and remaining cognitively flexible. Students with this profile need a bridge from traditional special education to constructivist learning experiences. We may summarize these differing views as in Table 9.3.

The Bridge Model

Many students with disabilities do not benefit from either the medical model or the constructivist one until they have the tools necessary to learn. The learning strategies model is a middle ground on this continuum and was designed, ideally, so that students could initiate their own learning; sustain attention for complex, multistep tasks; form hypotheses; and evaluate their own performance. Although there are many kinds of learning strategy models, perhaps the easiest and most practical of these approaches is Bonnie Camp's *Think Aloud* Program. The *Think Aloud* Program is designed to increase student self-control by the explicit teaching of self-talk strategies for solving a range of problems. Because many children with disabilities lack verbal mediation skills, this is a natural step to move them toward constructivist activity. You can easily incorporate this into whole-class instruction. You would simply introduce four questions students can ask themselves as they set about to learn. They involve

- identifying problems ("What am I to do?" "How can I find out?");
- choosing a plan or strategy ("How can I do it? What are some plans?");

TABLE 9.3 A Comparison of Approaches in Special Education

Criteria for Classifying Instruction	Medical Model Special Education	The Bridge: Learning Strategy Model	Constructivist Special Education
Pace of learning	Carefully controlled by teacher	Initially controlled by teacher. As student masters use of self-questioning, control turned over to student	Controlled by student
Sequence of learning	Prescribed by commercially available system	Teacher	Based on consultation between student and teacher
Selection of materials	Controlled by teacher or prescribed by curriculum	Teacher	Selected and/or created by student
Way student spends time	Student is active but frequently on drill and rote learning of restricted content in particular academic domains, usually in response to teacher directions and/or requests	Teacher presents problems. Student practices self-questioning and problem-solving strategies	Student produces material, teaches others, or frames questions. Often in nontraditional activities (music, art, construction)
Way of confirming and acknowledging learning	Teacher, or results of standardized testing, determines when, and how much, learning has occurred	Initially, teacher. As student masters self-questioning through (guided) practice and the use of appropriate problem-solving strategies, student	Production of artifacts and their collection (e.g., in portfolios), demonstrations, performances, and community activity

- self-monitoring ("Am I using my plan?"); and
- self-evaluation ("Is my plan working? How did I do? Do I need a new plan?").

When students use these questions in the context of the curriculum (and not separate from it), together with a menu of problem-solving strategies (such as brainstorming, means-end analysis, mnemonic memory strategies, etc.), they quickly acquire a wide repertoire of powerful learning tools.

Powerful Ideas for Inclusive Classrooms

Buddy Systems or the Value of Teaching Others

Revisiting Jan's Classroom

Ironically, perhaps one of the most powerful learning approaches for students with disabilities is to prepare them to teach others. We observed this (and it was dramatic) very recently in Jan Carpenter's classroom. Steve, a student with severe attentional and organizational difficulties, typically arrived unprepared for school—he rarely arrived with his books or writing utensils, had difficulty settling down for class work, and often appeared confused shortly after directions had been given. Many special educators and proponents of collaborative groups emphasize the importance of pairing students like Steve with academically advanced students who can model appropriate classroom and social behaviors. Jan chose a seemingly counterintuitive approach and paired Steve with a student whose organizational skills were weaker than his own. After a variety of interventions that often resulted in Steve becoming upset and Jan becoming frustrated, she asked Steve if he could help a student with mild autism named Maria to get organized in the morning, to keep her materials tidy, and to remember to bring her books home for homework assignments. On the first day of Steve's "teaching," Steve approached Maria at the end of the school day and asked the following questions: "Maria, what do you need to do to make sure you have everything you need? How can you remember to bring these materials home? What will you do tomorrow morning to remember to bring your homework to school?"

Jan's strategy worked brilliantly. Steve began to rehearse verbally the very strategies and questions he needed to ask himself to become more focused, responsible, and engaged with school assignments. For the first time, Steve began to feel empowered, as if learning was something within his control. For the first time, Steve saw at first hand the value of self-questioning, of teaching, and of collaborating with another. Finally, Steve became a model for Maria, and slowly she began to learn. Who might she teach next?

Accommodations

For most students who are eligible for special education service, disabilities are life span issues. The ways in which they approach material, the challenges they face, and the compensatory strategies they use—all these things are unlikely to change over time. If students are struggling in your class, this means it is imperative (because students are unlikely to change) that you think about the ways in which challenged students can fit into the environment without affecting your other students. How is this possible? Many years ago, one of us was involved in a consultation with a 10th-grade chemistry teacher who complained that a hyperactive student in her class continually tapped his pencil on the lab table, disrupting her and other students. The teacher shared with us that most days ended with arguments (because the student would continue tapping moments after he was asked to stop) and an occasional angry exchange. From the teacher's point of view, it was unclear whether the tapping was a willful attempt to continually disrupt the classroom or a manifestation of a behavior out of the boy's control. Either way, the behavior had to stop. Thinking about this behavior as something that must be changed (i.e., thinking that the *student* must be changed) is a mindset that guarantees teacher frustration and anger, student resentment, and very often feelings of inferiority and impotence in both. One way to frame this dilemma is the following: The student *needs* to tap, and the teacher *needs* a distraction-free environment. Accepting for a moment that both are in fact true needs (and that the student is not simply trying to be difficult), are these needs mutually exclusive? Of course not. Readers who already have begun to think about how we can change the environment and not the student already know this. For the rest of you, the solution to this dilemma can be found at the end of the chapter.

What About Fairness?

Unfortunately, many teachers believe that accommodating an individual student need is somehow unfair to other students. As Richard Lavoie has elegantly pointed out on his well-known video about the F.A.T. city workshop (1989), it is not about the *other* students! Lavoie points out that a teacher who fails to make accommodations to a student with a disability because she feels she may be unfair to the others is using the same logic as a teacher skilled in CPR who refuses to administer resuscitation to a student who collapses in the middle of her room because she doesn't have time to administer CPR to *all* the students in her room. Obviously, all the students do not need CPR. Fairness is about need.

Ignore Bloom's Taxonomy

If you're a preservice teacher, it's probably too late to try to forget Bloom after the amount of time you've spent hearing about his hierarchy of learning. For many students with disabilities, however, Bloom simply needs to be ignored if you are to facilitate learning. When we think about constructivist classrooms, whether or not they include students like Sam from our fable in Chapter 5 (and almost every classroom does), we need to focus on how individual students learn—not on a predetermined sequence or hierarchy that is perhaps true for some students. "Some students" are not *your* students. Your students will differ in many ways, and you must follow their lead, their needs, and their strengths. Many students may, for example, be able to make informed judgments (Bloom: "evaluate") about Plato's ideas—even though they may not be able to read or remember (Bloom: "knowledge") specific factual information about how to spell his name, when he lived, or where he was from. Similarly, many students are ready for sophisticated mathematical concepts despite being unable to perform simple calculations.

Tough Questions

1. Should all students, regardless of the severity of disability, be educated in regular classrooms? Why? Why not?

2. At what age, if ever, should a decision be made that a student should pursue vocational preparation instead of a more academically based education? Who should be involved in such a decision?

3. Is there a value to labeling students? Why? Why not?

4. Given the projected increases in the number of Spanish-speaking students, should learning Spanish be required of all new teachers? Why or why not?

5. Should students learn about cultural diversity issues even if they live in regions of the country that are fairly homogeneous? If so, given the lack of diversity in the area, what would be the context for learning?

6. Should the makeup of your classroom, school, or district have some bearing on curriculum requirements? That is, should schools emphasize more of an international perspective when establishing standards for the study of literature, art, history, and other subjects, or should we continue to focus on the contributions of Europeans and North Americans?

7. What will you do if, like Susan Jackson, you get a new teaching job and have trouble with *teacher* difference? How will you resolve conflicts?

The Pen-Tapping Dilemma

A rubber pad was placed on the lab table, allowing the student to tap to his heart's content without disturbing his classmates or the teacher.

Ten

Redemption
and Bon Voyage

Where Is Susan Jackson Now?

When we left Susan Jackson in Chapter 1, she was crying on the floor of an 8th-grade public school classroom, ready to resign. Did she? It's time to read the rest of her letter.

I asked Reggie to get the principal because I really was going to resign. There was this little part of me that wanted to stay, but there was this great big dinosaur sized part of me that just wanted to run away. The principal came down and I was a complete hysterical mess and I just said, "I can't do this anymore. I thought I could, but I can't."

He listened to me and although he couldn't understand most of what I was saying because I was crying so hard, somehow when he was talking I stopped crying. He has that effect. He is one of those non-emotional people who always seems to be in control. I told him what Cindy and Elizabeth and John had said, and he basically said that whatever our differences in teaching philosophy, they were right. I am not their problem. My job is to teach language arts in my room with my students. They can't trust me to pull my weight on a team project until I prove that I can do my own thing in my own room. He also said that I expected to just walk in and be part of a team. He said, "You expect to go from step 1 to step 10 without going through steps 2 through 9, and you can't." He also said that if I chose to leave, it was going to be difficult for me to find a more supportive school (yeah, right).

I still hate Cindy and Elizabeth, but Mr. Schwartz was right about the teaming thing. Some wise words. I did somehow think without even knowing it that I would walk in and the team thing would just sort of magically materialize. When I got home, I called my mother (I call her almost every day, these days) and I told her what I was thinking. I was definitely in the deepest pit I have ever been in in my life. I just kept saying to her "I don't think I can go back. Oh God, I just don't think I can go back." The flight instinct was really working overtime. She kept saying that it was my decision, and she would support me, but if I left, I was going to be totally responsible for the financial repercussions of my decision.

There was no school the next day because the roads were icy (thank God for natural disasters), so I had an extra day off to really think about what I should do. The following day, I dragged myself to school, and on the way I decided that I had to turn to the students. So I did the Eliot Wigginton thing. I said to them, "OK, I spent the entire week thinking about you and the way things have been going in this class, and I don't like it. We are going to change some things here. First of all, we are going to have a discussion and in order to do that, what needs to happen?" Someone said that people needed to raise their hands to be called on. I agreed, and of course someone blurted something out immediately, so I stopped and said, "OK, there we go. If you have a question or a comment, please raise your hand." I sat cross-legged on the table (which seemed to throw them a bit) and, by God, we had a great class discussion in all four classes. At some point in my second class discussion we got on the topic of rewards (the students brought it up). One student said that he really liked it when teachers gave out little incentives like candy, so I said, "So, what do the rest of you think about that?"

About four students raised their hands and I called on Tanika, one of the most mature students I have. She said, "I don't think we should have to be bribed to learn. We should want to learn just because we should want to learn."

I could have kissed her.

Then about six or seven other students agreed. Joe, a student who is just kind of your average Joe, said, "I think teachers just think we won't do anything unless they give us some kind of reward, but I think we do want to learn, but sometimes we forget because we are so used to getting stuff."

Then Saul, who has an IEP for language, said, "Yeah, but learning is harder for some people. And I know that people make fun of me because I go to Ms. Washington (the special education aide) for extra help, but I don't care because I need the help and maybe learning is rewarding for some of you but it's really hard for me and sometimes that little extra something at the end keeps me trying." He spoke with such passion and so articulately that everyone just sat there stunned for a second, and then the class applauded. They clapped for

him because he had been brave enough to tell the truth and expose himself,
and that was so brave.

Looking back, I guess it was at that moment that I realized that I could do
it—just because my students were so great.

—Susan

In Chapter 1 you met Susan Jackson, a highly skilled, confident young teacher with big dreams and early disappointments. Now, the excitement she feels, as students' voices come alive and renew her hopes, overshadows Susan's initial unhappiness, her conflicts with team members, and her struggle to make it happen in her classroom. Susan is at the beginning of her journey and at a major turning point. Not all, or not even most, of her issues have been settled. She will need to work at communicating with the other teachers as well as with the students and parents. One class period can make a huge difference in the dynamics of a classroom and in the dynamics of student learning, but creating and sustaining a constructivist classroom takes continual diligence, reflection, a strong vision, and a willingness to keep trying.

You have also met Jan Carpenter, Ann Lipsitt, Janette Roberts, and Katy Smith. Each of these teachers and hundreds more around the nation travel on different paths and arrive in different places. Like others who leave behind safe and familiar, yet deeply unsatisfying, places for more promising territories, each of these teachers travels now with high hopes, positive energy, and yes, an incomplete map. If you made it to the end of this book, it is a journey and adventure you are ready to begin as well.

Creating and Sustaining the Constructivist Classroom is meant to be a sort of compass to help you find your bearings and stay the course on what promises to be a challenging, lifelong voyage. By now, you know that there will be obstacles, detours, bumpy roads, and periodic occasions that may make you feel as if you are out of gas. Refer to this book as you need to, and remember that to sustain your thoughts, efforts, and changes, you will need to spend time reflecting and developing and re-developing your own compass; remember also to help your students create and develop the tools they need for their own excursions. Review the challenge statements near the end of Chapter 2 and the Tough Questions throughout the book at each transition you make. We are confident that it is the journey itself that holds the key to learning for you and your students.

We leave you with words from Don Christensen (personal communication, January 31, 1997), yet another teacher who has forged his own route:

> You cannot motivate others, it is true, but you can inspire them; you can reach those inner thoughts and questions and touch those raw nerves and weave enough magic for you all so that the active process is engaged.

It is time for you to go and weave some magic for yourself and your students. Bon voyage! Write to us by e-mail (Marloweb@ badger.jsc.vsc.edu or Pagem@badger.jsc.vsc.edu) or join us at our Web site (The International Center for Constructivist Classroom Teachers) and tell us what your journey is like. We will keep you posted about Susan.

Tough Questions

We close this chapter and our book with some more tough questions for you to consider, debate, and struggle with, courtesy of our heroine Susan Jackson.

1. Did Mr. Schwartz, the principal, handle the situation appropriately? Was he supportive of Susan? Did he send her the right message? What else could he have done?

2. How can you balance factors such as individual and special student needs, predetermined curriculum requirements, time constraints, parental concerns, the need for high standardized test scores, and a myriad of other issues and still structure the classroom so students have the opportunity to discover knowledge for themselves?

3. If you have only 40 minutes per day (35 after attendance), have five students in each class who are on IEPs and who need extensive individual attention, face a group of parents of which half are lobbying for a "back to the basics" curriculum, have many students who will soon be taking the SATs and

their parents will "kill them" if they don't score over 1,100, and are in a district that says you have to study the economic structure of Canada even though no one, including you, cares about it, how constructivist can you be?

4. How student-centered can learning be in a high school system that does not provide for or allow flexible scheduling, team teaching, and opportunities for learning outside the school's walls?

5. How can you provide a forum for an integrated and cohesive learning experience if you see the students for only one of the nine periods per day?

6. How can you "get around" all those rules and regulations that seem to have nothing to do with students really *learning* anything, such as the "grade a week" rule, or "all students will have 40 minutes of English homework every night no matter what"?

7. How can a new teacher introduce new ideas to team members without causing friction?

8. How can one teacher make effective changes in a school that does not accommodate change?

9. What are some of the first steps a teacher could or should take before introducing changes to a class or school in order to establish the most positive environment and the best chance for change?

References

Aiken, W. M. (1942). *The story of the Eight Year Study* (Vol. 1). New York: Harper & Brothers.

Association for Supervision and Curriculum Development. (1995, Summer). Reinventing science education. *Curriculum Update,* pp. 1-8.

Atwell, N. (1987). *In the middle: Writing, reading and learning with adolescents.* Upper Montclair, NJ: Bynton/Cook.

Ausubel, D. P. (1968). *Educational psychology: A cognitive view.* New York: Holt, Rinehart & Winston.

Barry, N. H., & Lechner, J. V. (1995). Preservice teachers' attitudes about and awareness of multicultural teaching and learning. *Teaching and Teacher Education, 11*(2), 149-161.

Beane, J. A. (1993). *A middle school curriculum: From rhetoric to reality.* Columbus, OH: National Middle School Association.

Booth, M. (1980). A modern world history course and the thinking of adolescent pupils. *Education Review, 32,* 245-257.

Boyer, E. L. (1983). *High school: A report on secondary education in America.* New York: Harper and Row.

Boyer, E. L. (1988). *Report card on school reform.* New York: The Carnegie Foundation for the Advancement of Teaching.

Bredderman, T. (1983). Effects of activity-based elementary science on student outcomes: A quantitative synthesis. *Review of Educational Research, 53*(4), 449-518.

Brimm, R. P. (1963). *The junior high school.* New York: The Center for Applied Research in Education.

Brodhagen, B., Weilbacher, G., & Beane, J. (1992). Living in the future: An experiment with an integrative curriculum. *Dissemination Service on the Middle Grades, 23*(9), 1-7.

Bruner, J. S. (1961). The act of discovery. *Harvard Educational Review,* *31*(1), 21-32.

Bruner, J. S. (1971). *The relevance of education.* New York: W. W. Norton & Co.

Burrello, L. C., Burrello, J. M., & Winninger, J. (1995). *A learner centered school* [Video series]. Bloomington: Indiana University, Radio and Television Services.

Campbell, H. M. (1971). *John Dewey.* New York: Twayne.

Canady, R. L., & Rettig, M. D. (1996). *Teaching in the block: Strategies for engaging active learners.* Princeton, NJ: Eye on Education.

Carnegie Council on Adolescent Development. (1989). *Turning points: Preparing American youth for the 21st century.* New York: Carnegie Corporation of New York.

Carnine, D. (1994). Introduction to the mini series: Diverse learners and prevailing, emerging, and research-based educational approaches and their tools. *School Psychology Review, 23*(3), 341-350.

Clarke, J. H., & Agne, R. M. (1997). *Interdisciplinary high school teaching: Strategies for integrated learning.* Boston: Allyn & Bacon.

Clinchy, E. (1994). Higher education: The albatross around the neck of our public schools. *Phi Delta Kappan, 75*(10), 744-751.

Collier, J. J., Laatsch, M., & Ferrero, P. (1972). *Film analysis of the Rough Rock Community school—phase one.* (Manuscript on file at Rough Rock, Chinle, AZ)

Commager, H. S. (1980). *The study and teaching of history.* Columbus, OH: C. E. Merrill.

Conley, D. T. (1996). Where's Waldo? The conspicuous absence of higher education from school reform and one state's response. *Phi Delta Kappan, 78*(4), 309-314.

Connell, W. F. (1980). *A history of education in the twentieth century world.* New York: Teachers College Press.

Cuban, L. (1983). How did teachers teach, 1890-1980? *Theory Into Practice, 22*(3), 159-165.

Cuban, L. (1990). Reforming again, again and again. *Educational Researcher, 19*(1), 3-13.

Darling-Hammond, L. (1993). Reframing the school reform agenda: Developing capacity for school transformation. *Phi Delta Kappan, 74*(10), 752-761.

Dewey, J. (1916). *Democracy and education.* New York: Macmillan.

Dewey, J. (1933). *How we think.* Boston: D. C. Heath.

Dewey, J. (1970). *The way out of educational confusion.* Westport, CT: Greenwood. (Original work published 1931)

Dewey, J. (1972). *Experience and education*. New York: Collier Books. (Original work published 1938)

Donmoyer, R. (1996). This issue: A focus on learning. *Educational Researcher, 25*(4), 4.

Ernst, F. (1953). How dangerous is John Dewey. *Atlantic Monthly, 191*(5), 59-62.

Freire, P. (1974). *Pedagogy of the oppressed*. New York: Seabury.

Freire, P. (1981). *Education for critical consciousness*. New York: Continuum.

Gardner, H. (1983). *Frames of mind: The theory of multiple intelligences*. New York: Basic Books.

Gardner, H. (1993). *Multiple intelligences: The theory in practice*. New York: Basic Books.

George, P. S., Stevenson, C., Thomason, J., & Beane, J. (1992). *The middle school—and beyond*. Alexandria, VA: Association for Supervision and Curriculum Development.

Goodlad, J. I. (1984). *A place called school: Prospects for the future*. New York: McGraw-Hill.

Gray, P., & Chanoff, D. (1986, February). Democratic schooling: What happens to young people who have charge of their own education? *American Journal of Education*, pp. 182-213.

Greene, K. B. (1942). Activity education. *Review of Educational Research, 12*(3), 280-288.

Hartoonian, M. (1984). *Computers and social knowledge: Opportunities and opportunity cost*. (ERIC Document Reproduction Service No. ED 247 202)

Heinich, R., Molenda, M., Russell, J. D., & Smaldino, S. (1996). *Instructional media and technologies for learning* (5th ed.). Englewood Cliffs, NJ: Prentice Hall.

Henley, M., Ramsey, R. S., & Algozzine, R. (1993). *Characteristics of and strategies for teaching students with mild disabilities*. Boston: Allyn & Bacon.

Hodgkinson, H. L. (1992). *A demographic look at tomorrow*. Washington, DC: Institute for Educational Leadership Center for Demographic Policy.

Hodgkinson, H. L. (1993). American education: The good, the bad, and the task. *Phi Delta Kappan, 84*(8), 619-623.

Jenness, D. (1990). *Making sense of social studies*. New York: Macmillan.

Juel, C. (1988). Learning to read and write: A longitudinal study of fifty-four children from first through fourth grade. *Journal of Educational Psychology, 80*(4), 437-447.

Kersh, B. Y. (1962). The motivating effect of learning by directed discovery. *Journal of Educational Psychology, 53*(2), 65-71.

Kilpatrick, W. H. (1918). The project method. *Teachers College Record, 19*, 319-351.

Kilpatrick, W. H. (1929). *How we learn: The psychological basis of the project method.* Calcutta: Association Press.

Kilpatrick, W. H. (1969). The new adult education. In W. H. Kilpatrick (Ed.), *The educational frontier* (pp. 122-159). New York: Arno Press and The New York Times. (Original work published 1933)

Kohn, A. (1993). *Punished by rewards: The trouble with gold stars, incentive plans, A's, praise, and other bribes.* Boston: Houghton Mifflin.

Kohn, A. (1996). Grading performance assessments. *Education Update, 38*(8), 4-5.

Kugelmass, J. W. (1995). Educating children with learning disabilities in Foxfire classrooms. *Journal of Learning Disabilities, 28*(9), 545-553.

Labinowicz, E. (1980). *The Piaget primer: Thinking, learning, teaching.* Menlo Park, CA: Addison-Wesley.

Lavoie, R. (1989). *Understanding learning disabilities: Frustration, anxiety, tension, the F.A.T. city workshop* (produced by Peter Rosen for Eagle Hill School Outreach). Alexandria, CA: PBS Video.

Levin, R. J. (1987). *Technology in the curriculum.* Chelmsford, MA: Merrimack Education Center.

Lewis, A. C. (1990). Tracking the national goals. *Phi Delta Kappan, 72*(7), 496-506.

Lipsitz, J. (1984). *Successful schools for young adolescents.* New Brunswick, NJ: Transaction.

Lyon, G. R. (1995, August). *Dyslexia.* Paper presented at Disabilities: Unifying Services Across the Lifespan, Johnson, VT.

MacInnis, C., & Hemming, H. (1995). Linking the needs of students with learning disabilities to a whole language curriculum. *Journal of Learning Disabilities, 28*(9), 535-544.

MacKenzie, A. A., & White, R. T. (1982). Fieldwork in geography and long term memory structures. *American Educational Research Journal, 19*(4), 623-632.

Marlowe, B. A. (1990). *Identifying learning disabilities in the deaf population.* Unpublished doctoral dissertation, Catholic University of America, Washington, D.C.

Massialas, B. G., & Zevin, J. (1967). *Creative encounters in the classroom: Teaching and learning through discovery.* New York: John Wiley & Sons.

McCarty, T. L., Lynch, R. H., Wallace, S., & Benally, A. (1991). Classroom inquiry and Navajo learning styles: A call for reassessment. *Anthropology and Education Quarterly, 22*(1), 42-59.

McLuhan, M. (1967). *The medium is the massage, by Marshall McLuhan and Quentin Fiore* (coordinated by Jerome Agel). New York: Random House.

Middle Grade Task Force. (1987). *Caught in the middle. The task of educational reform for young adolescents in California schools.* Sacramento, CA: California State Department of Public Instruction.

National Academy of Sciences. (1996). *National education standards.* Washington, DC: Department of Education. (ERIC Document Reproduction Service No. ED 391 690)

National Association of Secondary School Principals. (1985). *An agenda for excellence at the middle level.* Reston, VA: National Association of Secondary School Principals.

National Association of Secondary School Principals. (1996). *Breaking ranks: Changing an American institution* (Report of the National Association of Secondary School Principals in Partnership with the Carnegie Foundation for the Advancement of Teaching in the High Schools of the 21st Century). Alexandria, VA: Association for Supervision and Curriculum Development. (ERIC Document Reproduction Service No. ED 393 205).

National Center for History in the Schools. (1994). *National standards for United States History: Exploring the American experience.* Los Angeles, CA: Author.

National Center for History in the Schools. (1996). *National standards for history. Basic edition.* Los Angeles, CA: Author. (ERIC Document Reproduction Service No. ED 391 690)

National Commission on Social Studies in the Schools. (1989). *Charting a course: Social studies for the 21st century: A report of the Curriculum Task Force of the National Commission on Social Studies in the Schools.* Washington, DC: Author. (ERIC Document Reproduction Service No. ED 317 450)

National Council of Teachers of English and International Reading Association. (1996). *Standards for the English language arts.* Urbana, IL: National Council of Teachers of English, and Newark, DE: International Reading Association.

National Council of Teachers of Mathematics. (1992). *Curriculum and evaluation standards for school mathematics.* Reston, VA: Author.

National Council of Teachers of Mathematics. (1995). *Assessment standards for school mathematics.* Reston, VA: Author.

National History Day, Inc. (1986). *National History Day contest guide.* Cleveland: Author.

NMSA Resolutions Committee. (1989). National Middle School Association 1988-89 resolutions. *Middle School Journal, 20*(3), 18-20.

O'Neil, J. (1995). Teachers and technology: Potential and pitfalls. *Educational Leadership, 53*(2), 10-12.

O'Neil, J. (1996). On surfing—and steering—the net: A conversation with Clifford Stoll. *Educational Leadership, 54*(3), 12-17.

Office of Technology Assessment. (1995). *Teachers and technology: Making the connection.* Washington, DC: Government Printing Office.

Page, M. (1990). *Active learning: Historical and contemporary perspectives.* Unpublished manuscript, University of Massachusetts—Amherst. (ERIC Document Reproduction Service No. ED 338389).

Page, M. (1992). *National History Day: An ethnohistorical case study.* Unpublished doctoral dissertation, University of Massachusetts, Amherst.

Papert, S. (1980). *Mindstorms: Children, computers, and powerful ideas.* New York: Basic Books.

Pestalozzi, J. H. (1898). *How Gertrude teaches her children* (L. E. Holland & F. C. Turner, Trans.). New York: C. E. Bardeen. (Original work published 1801)

Phillips, G., & Faris, R. (1977). Learning as much in different ways at an action learning high school. *Phi Delta Kappan, 59,* 133.

Piaget, J. (1971). *Biology and knowledge: An essay on the relation between organic regulations and cognitive processes.* Chicago: University of Chicago Press. (Original work published 1967)

Piaget, J. (1995). Essay on the theory of qualitative values in static sociology. In J. Piaget (Ed.), *Sociological studies* pp. 97-133. New York: Routledge. (Original work published 1941)

Plimpton, G. (1989). Graduation speech, Tabor Academy, Marion, Massachusetts.

Postman, N., & Weingartner, C. (1969). *Teaching as a subversive activity.* New York: Dell.

Prawat, R. S. (1992, May). Teachers' beliefs about teaching and learning: A constructivist perspective. *American Journal of Education,* pp. 354-389.

Puckett, J. L. (1986). *Foxfire reconsidered: A critical ethnohistory of a twenty-year experiment in progressive education.* Unpublished doctoral dissertation, University of North Carolina, Chapel Hill.

Puckett, J. L. (1989). *Foxfire reconsidered: A twenty year experiment in progressive education*. Chicago: University of Illinois Press.

Rousseau, J.-J. (1957). *Emile* (B. Foxley, Trans.). New York: E. P. Dutton & Co. (Original work published 1762)

Rusk, R. R. (1956). *The philosophical bases of education*. Boston: Houghton Mifflin.

Saettler, P. (1968). *A history of instructional technology*. New York: McGraw-Hill.

Sahakian, M. L., & Sahakian, W. S. (1974). *Rousseau as educator*. New York: Twayne.

Secules, T., Cottom, C., Bray, M., & Miller, L. (1997). Creating schools for thought. *Educational Leadership, 56*(6), 56-59.

Sharan, S. (1985). Cooperative learning effects on ethnic relations and achievement in Israeli junior high school classrooms. In R. Slavin (Ed.), *Learning to cooperate, cooperating to learn* (pp. 313-344). New York: Plenum Press.

Sharan, S., & Shachar, H. (1988). *Language and learning in the cooperative classroom*. New York: Springer-Verlag.

Sharan, S., & Sharan, Y. (1976). *Small group teaching*. Englewood Cliffs, NJ: Educational Technology Publications.

Sharan, S., & Sharan, Y. (1989/1990). Group investigation expands cooperative learning. *Educational Leadership, 47*(4), 17-21.

Sharan, S., & Sharan, Y. (1992). *Expanding cooperative learning through group investigation*. New York: Teachers College Press.

Shaywitz, S. (1995, July). *Implications of the Connecticut longitudinal study*. Paper presented at Disabilities: Unifying Services Across the Lifespan, Johnson, VT.

Shemilt, D. (1980). Those who understand: Knowledge growth in teaching. *Educational Researcher, 15*, 4-14.

Sileo, T. W., Sileo, S. P., & Prater, M. A. (1996, January). Parent and professional partnerships in special education: Multicultural considerations. *Intervention in School and Clinic*, pp. 145-153.

Simon, P. (1973). Kodachrome. *There Goes Rhymin' Simon* [Record album]. New York: Columbia.

Sizer, T. (1984). *Horace's compromise: The dilemma of the American high school*. Boston: Houghton Mifflin.

Sizer, T. (1996). *Horace's hope*. Boston: Houghton Mifflin.

Slavin, R. E. (1989). Cooperative learning and student achievement. In R. Slavin (Ed.), *School and classroom organization* (pp. 129-158). Englewood Cliffs, NJ: Lawrence Erlbaum.

Sless, D. (1981). *Learning and visual communication*. London: Croom Helm.

Smilovitz, R. (1996). *If not now, when? Education not schooling*. Kearney, NE: Morris.

Smith, K. (1993). Becoming the "guide on the side." *Educational Leadership, 51*(2), 35-37.

Stecker, E. (1987). *Slide showmanship*. New York: Amphoto.

Steinberg, L. (1996). *Beyond the classroom: Why school reform has failed and what parents need to do*. New York: Simon & Schuster.

Turnbull, A. P., Turnbull, H. R., Shank, M., & Leal, D. (1995). *Exceptional lives: Special education in today's schools*. Englewood Cliffs, NJ: Prentice Hall.

Tyler, R. (1975). Educational benchmarks in retrospect: Educational change since 1915. *Viewpoints, 51*(2), 11-30.

Vermont Middle Grades Task Force. (1991). *The middle matters: Transforming education for Vermont's young adolescents*. Montpelier: Vermont Department of Education.

Walten, N. E., & Travers, R. M. (1963). Analysis and investigation of teaching methods. In N. L. Gage (Ed.), *Handbook of research on teaching* (pp. 448-505). Chicago: Rand McNally.

Washburne, C., & Raths, L. (1927). The high school achievement of children trained under the individual technique. *Elementary School Journal, 28*, 214-224.

Weil, M. L., & Murphy, J. (1982). Instruction process. In H. E. Mitzel (Ed.), *Encyclopedia of educational research* (Vol. 2, pp. 890-917). New York: Free Press.

Wigginton, E. (1985). *Sometimes a shining moment: The Foxfire experience*. New York: Anchor Press/Doubleday.

Wigginton, E. (1989). *Foxfire* grows up. *Harvard Educational Review, 59*(1), 24-49.

Will, M. (1985, December). Keynote address. Presented at the Wingspread Conference on The Education of Special Needs Students: Research Findings and Implications for Policy and Practice, Racine, WI.

Worthen, B. R. (1968). Discovery and expository task presentation in elementary mathematics. *Journal of Educational Psychology Monograph, 59*(1).

Ysseldyke, J. E., & Algozzine, R. (1995). *Special education: A practical approach for teachers* (3rd ed.). Boston: Houghton Mifflin.

Additional Readings

Association for Supervision and Curriculum Development. (1996). Making a case for democratic schools. *Education Update, 38*(3), 1, 3.

Au, K. H. (1979). Participation structures in a reading lesson with Hawaiian children: Analysis of a culturally appropriate instructional event. *Anthropology and Education Quarterly, 11*, 91-114.

Blake, D. W. (1981). Observing children learning history. *The History Teacher, 14*, 533-549.

Brooks, J. G., & Brooks, M. G. (1993). *In search of understanding: The case for constructivist classrooms.* Alexandria, VA: Association for Supervision and Curriculum Development.

Caine, R. N., & Caine, G. (1997). *Education on the edge of possibility.* Alexandria, VA: Association for Supervision and Curriculum Development.

Carr, W., & Hartnett, A. (1996). *Education and the struggle for democracy: The politics of educational ideas.* Buckingham, UK: Open University Press.

DeVries, R., & Zan, B. (1994). *Moral classrooms, moral children: Creating a constructivist atmosphere in early education.* New York: Teachers College Press.

Downey, M. T., & Levstik, L. S. (1991). Teaching and learning history. In J. Shaver (Ed.), *Handbook of research on social studies teaching and learning: NCSS* (pp. 400-410). New York: Macmillan.

Geyer, D. L. (1936). The results of activity instruction: An interpretation of published findings. *Journal of Educational Research, 30*(3), 188-197.

Kagan, S. (1985). Co-op, Co-op: A flexible cooperative learning technique. In R. Slavin (Ed.), *Learning to cooperate, cooperating to learn* (pp. 277-312). New York: Plenum.

Meier, D. (1995). *The power of their ideas: Lessons for America from a small school in Harlem.* Boston: Beacon.

Moran, L. (1989). Some are more equal than others. In L. Moran (Ed.), *What's noteworthy on school improvement* (pp. 32-37). Wichita, KS: Mid Continent Educational Lab.

National Council of Teachers of Mathematics. (1991). *Professional standards for teaching mathematics.* Reston, VA: Author.

Noordhoff, K., & Kleinfeld, J. (1993). Preparing teachers for multicultural classrooms. *Teaching and Teacher Education, 9*(1), 27-39.

Puckett, J. (1989). Who wrote Foxfire: A consideration of ethnohistorical method. *Journal of Research and Development in Education, 22*(3), 71-78.

Salmon, P. (1995). *Psychology in the classroom: Reconstructing teachers and learners.* London: Cassell.

Zemelman, S., Daniels, H., & Hyde, A. A. (1993). *Best practice.* Portsmouth, NH: Heinemann.

Index

CORWIN
PRESS

The Corwin Press logo—a raven striding across an open book—represents the happy union of courage and learning. We are a professional-level publisher of books and journals for K–12 educators, and we are committed to creating and providing resources that embody these qualities. Corwin's motto is "Success for All Learners."